A Journey into
Dorothy Parker's
New York

SECOND EDITION

A Journey into
Dorothy Parker's
New York
Second Edition

Kevin C. Fitzpatrick

With a foreword by
Marion Meade

ArtPlace Series

Roaring Forties Press
Berkeley, California

Roaring Forties Press
1053 Santa Fe Avenue
Berkeley, California 94706

Printed in the United States of America.

Cataloging-in-Publication Data

Fitzpatrick, Kevin C., 1966-
   A journey into Dorothy Parker's New York, second edition / Kevin C. Fitzpatrick ; with a
foreword by Marion Meade.
   p. cm.
   ISBN 978-1-938901-07-2 (pbk)
   ISBN 978-1-938901-08-9 (pdf)
   ISBN 978-1-938901-09-6 (e-pub)
   ISBN 978-1-938901-10-2 (Kindle)
   Includes bibliographical references and index.

1. Parker, Dorothy, 1893-1967 — Homes and haunts — New York (State) — New York. 2.
Parker, Dorothy, 1893-1967 — Knowledge — New York (N.Y.) 3. Authors, American —
Homes and haunts — New York (State) — New York. 4. Authors, American — 20th century
— Biography. 5. New York (N.Y.) — Intellectual life — 20th century. I. Meade, Marion. II.
Title.

PS3531.A5855 Z645 2013
818/.5209 — dc23

To Christina

Contents

Foreword

Some years ago I learned that young Dorothy Parker, while she was still Dorothy Rothschild, had lived in a rooming house at Broadway and 103rd Street. Exactly where was hard to say, after the passage of more than a half-century, but a combination of deduction and wishful thinking led me to situate her boardinghouse on the east side of Broadway, on the site of Lamstons five-and-ten.

Regrettably, the dime store is today a paint and wallpaper business. I myself was in the habit of nipping into Lamstons a few times a week because there are plenty of reasons to visit a five-and-dime, while the need for paint and wallpaper arises once or twice in a lifetime, if that. I suspect Dorothy Parker might have agreed because she had never been known to step foot in such an establishment. Saloons yes, paint stores no. Lamstons, I like to think, was her type of joint, a romantic emporium offering such essential wares of life as bobby pins and emergency Alka Seltzer.

If Dorothy Parker's spirit did not really frequent Lamstons—and I'm afraid it didn't—her association with countless other buildings is a documented fact. Should you think that a tour of her world must involve curiosities from a long-lost civilization, something equivalent to picture postcards of Pompeii and Herculaneum, you'd be wrong. What most startles me is how many of the buildings relating to her life still exist. Certain theaters—and those marvelous speakeasies—may have vaporized, but the Algonquin Hotel remains in the same spot, and a few doors down West 44th Street is the same office building where she found a job on *Vogue* in 1915. For that matter, the store in which she actually did buy her sundries, Zitomer's on Madison Avenue, is still thriving today.

With devotion and invention, Kevin C. Fitzpatrick has created a delicious illustrated guide to New York City and the doings of one of its legendary citizens. *A Journey into Dorothy Parker's New York* moves from the 1890s in the Upper West Side neighborhood where she lived until the age of twenty-seven, through the 1920s with its bootleg booze and jazz music, to the Cold War hysteria of the 1950s and the years beyond. The book offers chapters of literary and political history, popular culture, urban architecture, and theatrical lore, not to mention something else that is particularly fun to read: sidebars full of useful facts.

The last chapter traces Dorothy Parker's final years, when she made her home at the Volney, a quiet residential hotel on the Upper East Side. Frail and in poor health, she had trouble lifting her hands to the typewriter keys but continued writing whenever possible. One of her last pieces, published in Esquire in November 1964, paid tribute to the work of John Koch, a painter known for his elegant still lifes of well-bred New Yorkers. In "New York at 6:30 P.M.," she vividly reprised her intimate, bittersweet memories of that alluring hour of day, when the late afternoon sky was flushed "Renoir blue" and real fires were being lighted in real fireplaces. With a touch of sadness she noted, "There is no such hour on the present clock as 6:30, New York time. Yet, as only New Yorkers know, if you can get through the twilight, you'll live through the night."

For a glimpse into the heart and soul of the metropolis, for a chance to begin understanding those things that only New Yorkers know, the place to start is *A Journey into Dorothy Parker's New York*.

MARION MEADE

Preface to the Second Edition

When my publisher approached me about working on a second edition of this book, I thought long and hard about what to update. It had been seven years since the book was first published: during that time, I hadn't discovered any previously unknown apartments that Dorothy Parker had slept in. The 1900 immigration figures for New York City hadn't changed. I didn't buy her love letters on eBay. What could I update?

Quite a bit, as it turns out.

The story of Dorothy Parker and New York City continues to evolve. This became clear to me in 2012 as I descended a flight of dirty stairs inside the Algonquin Hotel. I say dirty not because the housekeeping staff was lax, but because the hotel was closed for five months for a massive renovation project. As a long-time fan of the Algonquin, I thought I knew a lot about it, or at least more than the casual devotee—until I took a private tour with General Manager Gary Budge and peered into the guts of the building, looking at steel and wood supports that nobody had laid eyes on since 1902. I decided to approach Dorothy Parker and her "journey" in a similar fashion as I prepared the second edition.

Since the publication of the first edition, building names and sites have changed. This was the first category I needed to update; as a licensed city tour guide, I can't send a visitor to the wrong address or to a business that is no longer operating. I spent an enjoyable few months verifying every address and business in the book.

Because I was visiting every location in the book, I decided to update many of the photos. This new edition contains seventy new photographs. But the revised images tell just part of a bigger story.

When I researched the first edition in the mid-2000s, not many vintage photos were available to the general public. Using archival photos of New York City and the personalities of the era that are now available, this edition presents a more layered tale of Mrs. Parker's time in Manhattan. Of particular note are the George Grantham Bain and the Detroit Publishing Company collections. These images, some more than one hundred years old, are as crisp as if they were taken last week.

Beyond the words and photos, the end of Dorothy Parker's story has also changed. At a dinner in Albany in 2011 at which she was inducted into the New York State Writers Hall of Fame, I was seated with fans of fellow inductees Herman Melville and Willa Cather (Mrs. Parker runs in good company). As the meal progressed, I heard about the Melville Society's museum and the Cather Foundation's hometown. By the time speeches and toasts were made, I was more than a little jealous of the other dead authors. Visitors to Pittsfield can see Melville's desk. In Red Cloud, Cather fans can visit houses, churches, an opera house—even an entire *prairie*—supported by her foundation. The Dorothy Parker Society—originally conceived of on the back of a taxi receipt—couldn't claim ownership of even a lamppost in Manhattan.

Later, back at home on the Upper West Side, I thought about the dozens of locations in this book. I recalled the hundreds of people I have led around Manhattan retracing Parker's footsteps. I took heart in the bronze plaques erected at her former homes, the new editions of her books that publishers keep issuing, the frequent amateur and professional productions based on Parker material presented around the world. Every member of the Writer's Hall of Fame is special, of course. But how special is Dorothy Parker? In Brooklyn, a distillery makes a gin named for her. The hottest club in São Paulo, Brazil, is Club Dorothy Parker. When New York City turned 400 in 2009, the Museum of the City of New York chose 400 people "who have helped define New York City for the past four centuries." Dorothy Parker claimed a place of honor in that list.

What has not changed since the first edition is the way that Dorothy Parker's view of the world resonates with readers, as so eloquently described by her foremost biographer, Marion Meade, in the foreword to this book. Author of *Dorothy Parker, What Fresh Hell Is This?*, Meade edited *The Portable Dorothy Parker: Complete Poems* and *The Ladies of the Corridor*. She lives and works on the Upper West Side, where she often considers the life of Mrs. Parker as she passes by many of the sites featured in this book.

Any fan of an author, musician, or movie enjoys exploring the locales that played a part in the life of the object of their passion. With *A Journey into Dorothy Parker's New York*, readers and travelers can retrace the life and times of Dorothy Parker while enjoying the best of past and present Manhattan.

A Journey into
Dorothy Parker's
New York
SECOND EDITION

Chapter I

Dorothy Parker

A Manhattan Confection

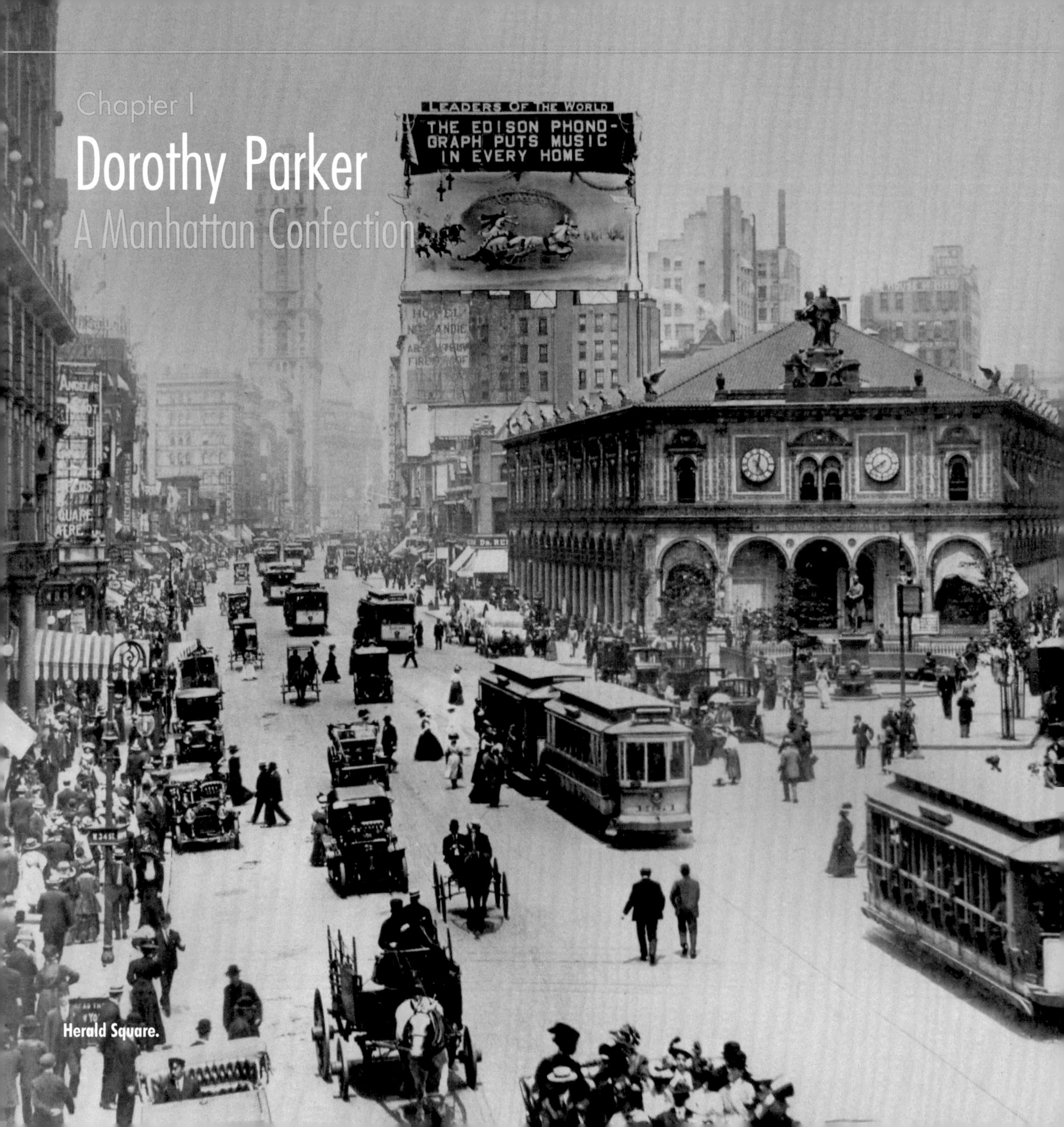
LEADERS OF THE WORLD
THE EDISON PHONO-
GRAPH PUTS MUSIC
IN EVERY HOME

Herald Square.

On the occasion of Dorothy Parker's fiftieth birthday in 1943, *Vogue* photographer George Platt Lynes created this portrait of her.

I t is the spring of 1988 and Dorothy Parker is back at the Algonquin Hotel, surrounded by reporters. A small crowd has gathered around the Round Table in the Round Table Room. Some have cocktails in hand; others are telling jokes; a few jot down quips and quotes in narrow reporters' notebooks. Television news cameras are rolling. Somewhere in the room, Mrs. Parker is waiting. She's in a can.

All eyes turn to the tall, white-haired Paul O'Dwyer as he moves to the front of the room with Dorothy Parker. The eighty-one-year-old lawyer from County Mayo, Ireland, had, with his late partner, Oscar Bernstien, built a law practice known throughout the city for representing underdogs, defending civil rights, and serving those in need. It was Bernstien who had drawn up Mrs. Parker's last will and testament. According to that will, after Parker's death in June 1967, her estate went to Dr. Martin Luther King Jr., a man she greatly admired but had never met. Ten months later he was assassinated, and Parker's literary rights were later transferred to the National Association for the Advancement of Colored People.

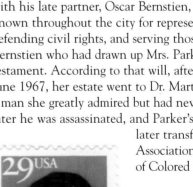

29 USA

Dorothy Parker
American Writer 1893-1967

Dorothy Parker's iconic status was officially recognized in 1992, when the U.S. Postal Service issued this commemorative stamp.

Mrs. Parker had been cremated in Westchester County, but her remains had gone unclaimed by her executrix, the playwright Lillian Hellman, and the ashes had been in O'Dwyer's filing cabinet for almost twenty years. Now the final chapter of Parker's life was being written—literally—by biographer Marion

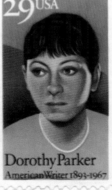

3

Dorothy's memorial in Baltimore.

brick memorial designed by Harry G. Robinson is meant to recall the Algonquin's Round Table. The memorial stands in a small grove of pines; pine needles and cones lie scattered on the grass. An urn containing Dorothy Parker's ashes stands in the center of the memorial, bearing a plaque commemorating her life and accomplishments. Always one to approach serious subjects with irreverence, Parker had tossed off a handful of mock epitaphs over the course of her life, but the real one reads:

> *Here lie the ashes of Dorothy Parker (1893–1967). Humorist, writer, critic, defender of human and civil rights. For her epitaph she suggested "Excuse My Dust." This memorial garden is dedicated to her noble spirit which celebrated the oneness of humankind, and to the bonds of everlasting friendship between black and Jewish people.*

Meade, who had discovered while researching her landmark biography *Dorothy Parker: What Fresh Hell Is This?* that the ashes had never been properly interred. O'Dwyer has called this press conference at the Algonquin to officially hand over Parker's ashes to Dr. Benjamin Hooks, executive director of the NAACP. After a short speech by O'Dwyer, Dr. Hooks graciously accepts the ashes and promises to create a proper memorial for this inveterate New Yorker. The irony is that Parker's final resting place will be at the NAACP headquarters in Baltimore, rather than in the city she had done so much to make famous.

On October 20, 1988, the ashes were placed in a garden outside the NAACP offices in Baltimore, with Dr. Hooks officiating over the dedication. The circular

After Mrs. Parker was finally laid to rest, a renewed interest in her work arose, as if quite literally from the ashes. Since the late 1980s, new collections of her work have been published and she has been the subject of four biographies, an award-winning Hollywood feature film, and an Oscar-winning documentary. In 1993 the U.S. Postal Service honored Parker with a commemorative postage stamp, and her birthplace in West End, New Jersey, was named a national literary landmark in 2005. The Dorothy Parker Society boasts nearly five thousand members around the world, offers monthly tours covering sites important to Dorothy Parker and the Algonquin Round Table, and hosts an annual "Parkerfest." Mrs. Parker herself might have commented on this activity with a typical sardonic observation, but no doubt she would also have been pleased with the upsurge of enthusiasm for her work, which has introduced many adoring fans to the Manhattan she called home.

Few other writers have portrayed any city with as much keen and insightful detail as Dorothy Parker did when writing of Manhattan. She belongs to an impressive club of New York City writers—Edith Wharton, Walt Whitman, Herman Melville, Zora Neale Hurston, J. D. Salinger—native sons and daughters who evoke, through their work, a city that is as alive and vibrant today as when they penned their words. In Dorothy Parker's New York, the speakeasies are always hopping, the party is just beginning, and all the taxicabs hold couples on their way to an *affaire de cœur*.

Dorothy Parker herself was a Manhattan confection: equal parts bootleg Scotch, Broadway lights, speakeasy smoke, skyscraper steel, streetcar noise, and jazz horns. She was a product of a city struggling economically but on the verge of enormous power and influence. Dorothy, the precocious offspring of a Jewish father and a Protestant mother, would not have been comfortable in turn-of-the-century Los Angeles, with its dirt roads

The Dorothy Parker Society on a tour of the New York Distilling Co. in Williamsburg, Brooklyn, which manufactures Dorothy Parker American Gin.

and deplorable culture. Chicago at the time was a cow town—a place of stockyards, not sophistication. And puritanical Boston certainly had no room for the likes of the future Mrs. Parker.

A Parker Portrait

In 1940, Pocket Books published *After Such Pleasures* in paperback. At the end of the collection of short stories, Dottie's editor added a brief biography and portrait of the author, then in her late forties:

Dorothy Parker is slightly over five feet in height, dark, and attractive, with somewhat weary eyes and a sad mouth. Her favorite possession is Robinson, a dachshund. She is superstitious, pessimistic, hates to be alone, and prefers to be considered a satirist rather than a humorist. She usually writes in longhand, crossing out every other word in order to achieve the utmost simplicity; she tries to avoid feminine style. Being extremely near-sighted, she wears glasses when writing, but she has never been seen on the street with them. Ernest Hemingway is her favorite author—flowers and a good cry are reported to be among her favorite diversions.

Script, typewriter, and pencil are props in this staged 1941 photo.

Only New York, with its bustling, crowded streets and undisputed role as the center of American popular culture, could have nurtured Dorothy, providing her access to and friendships with some of the most important cultural figures of the time. The life of Dorothy Parker is inescapably intertwined with the New York she inhabited; likewise, popular perception of New York and its history has been shaped by the life she lived and the world she captured in print.

Nineties New York: A City in Upheaval

At the end of the nineteenth century, New York was poised on the edge of tremendous economic, social, and political change. Dorothy was born into that world on August 22, 1893, in West End, New Jersey, at her family's summer beach cottage. That summer a catastrophic economic collapse launched a five-year depression in the United States. By the fall of 1893, 141 national banks had failed, followed by savings and loan institutions, mortgage companies, and private investment banks. Layoffs happened at an astonishing rate and only worsened during the freezing winter.

The same month that Eliza Rothschild delivered Dottie, Joseph Pulitzer's *New York World* announced a "war on hunger" and recounted tales of the indigent to its readers. Intrepid reporters Nellie Bly and Stephen Crane wrote first-person accounts of the city's downtrodden, including stories about mothers who couldn't feed their children and turned them out into the streets. While the Rothschilds slept, Pulitzer's newspaper wagons prowled the streets, handing out free loaves of bread.

The New York police canvassed homes door to door to assess the alarming situation, reporting 70,000 unemployed, of whom 25,000 were women. City officials offered little relief for the poor. City government, controlled by the corrupt Tammany Hall political machine, was starting to be overturned by the forces of good government, but it would take years for real moral and social reform to take effect. Against this backdrop, the population was exploding. In 1900 New York City had just over 3 million residents; in 1910, 4.8 million; by 1920 5.6 million people; and in 1930 more than 7 million—a 133 percent increase in just thirty years.

Although the Rothschilds, who were second-generation Americans, may not have felt much affinity for the newcomers from Europe overflowing the tenements on the Lower East Side, the newly arrived masses provided a dependable workforce. Some went to work for Henry

An estimated 12 million immigrants passed through Ellis Island, arriving on ships such as the S.S. *Imperator,* shown here.

Rothschild's garment business; others were employed as the family's household help. Dorothy never described what it was like inside her father's factory, but the use of sweatshop labor was so widespread that the working conditions there were quite likely poor and the pay minimal. In response to the harsh conditions, New York City soon became a hotbed for labor reform, with workers striking and thugs (and policemen) beating those in the picket lines. Child labor was an important issue, and women held strikes to protest intolerable working conditions for garment workers.

Women's rights, especially the right to vote, was another galvanizing issue of the day. When Dorothy was sixteen, more than 20,000 New York women wage earners went on strike for almost two months, and as she entered the writing profession in her early twenties, the suffrage movement was advocating voting rights for women. In October 1917 tens of thousands of women marched in a New York City suffrage parade. In June 1919 Congress proposed the Fifteenth Amendment, giving all citizens the right to vote regardless of sex; ratification was completed on August 18, 1920.

This was the world into which Dorothy Parker was born and from which she drew her inspiration. However, although she occasionally ventured into working-class lives with stories like "Clothe the Naked" and "The Standard of Living," she was much more at home chronicling the limited options available to middle-class women of the early twentieth century. In her verse, women are more likely to have their hearts broken by men than men are likely to be left heartbroken by women. In her fiction, she used stock characters for her female roles: doltish office girls, blushing new brides, flustered girlfriends, and society matrons who are small-minded or silly (and frequently both). Few of these women gain power or satisfaction from their interactions with the men in their lives.

Girls march in New York City in 1909 to protest child labor.

A poignant and powerful example is "Mr. Durant," written for *American Mercury* magazine in 1924. It's the tale of a loathsome middle-aged businessman who impregnates his twenty-year-old secretary. Dorothy's descriptions of the dress and mannerisms of the young female office worker are masterly for their portrayal from Mr. Durant's perspective: "When she bent over her work, her back showing white through her sleazy blouse, her clean hair coiled smoothly on her thin neck, her straight, childish legs crossed at the knee to support her pad, she had an undeniable appeal." As a Center Street trolley takes Mr. Durant uptown to his wife and children, he considers the dilemma with a cold, detached practicality:

> *As he had often jovially remarked to his friends, he knew "a thing or two." Cases like this could be what people of the world called "fixed up"—New York society women, he understood, thought virtually nothing of it. This case could be fixed up, too. He got Rose to go home, telling her not to worry; he would see that everything was all right. The main thing was to get her out of sight, with that nose and those eyes.*

The New York City of Dorothy Parker's imagination was one where women needed to be "fixed up" or simply removed from sight. Her fiction and poetry don't feature women transcending the roles that society had prescribed for them—none of her characters become powerful theater critics or social gadflies or Oscar-nominated Hollywood screenwriters.

Gin and Sin: Dottie Records the Jazz Age

Dorothy Parker was at her tantalizing best when she wrote about the apartment houses, afternoon teas, bridge games, train stations, and saloons that made up her New York life. She populated these settings with the unfaithful husbands, drunken social climbers, dissipated lovers, and cowardly gentlemen she saw around her. Yet the themes she worked and reworked continue to resonate today. Spouses are still unfaithful to each other; heartbreak and loss are forever part of the human condition; boneheaded bosses, insecure lovers, haughty neighbors, dull-witted children—no matter what decade these characters appear in, they will be understood. William Shakespeare had his conflicted princes, Parker her alcoholic debutantes, and both remain fresh and recognizable.

For a writer with Parker's remarkable talents, New York provided plenty of characters for fiction and poetry: bootleggers and stock traders, chorus girls and grandes dames, Fifth Avenue swells and the Bowery's down-and-outers. The years of relative peace between the First and Second World Wars gave Parker the freedom to write about affairs of the heart, the trials of suburbia, the inanities of social convention, and even the merits of gin versus scotch—topics that, in the hands of a trenchant observer such as Parker, not only made for timeless stories but sold magazines.

The printed word was enjoying heady days when Parker's career took off. The city had at least fifteen daily newspapers, with editions rolling off the presses in the morning and afternoon. With the addition of scores of magazines and cheap pulps and hundreds of dime novels, sidewalk newsstands were bursting with titles. Movies were still silent, radio was in its infancy, and live shows were the thing at the city's nearly eighty Broadway theaters (today there are about forty). Parker began her career at *Vogue*, which had transformed itself from printing dressmaking patterns to dictating style. When she joined *Vanity Fair*—the magazine was just four years old and already the most sophisticated publication in the country—she was minted as the reigning arbiter of sass and class. Her snappy wisecracks (dutifully retold by her ink-stained chums) and mordant verse (sent in to the most popular daily newspaper columnists) made her a symbol of the Roaring Twenties and an expert on Broadway, banter, and bacchanalia.

Although she did not draw the intense media scrutiny attracted by a couple like Scott and Zelda Fitzgerald, she was one of the best-known women of the time. Her reputation came primarily from her wisecracks and prose "squibs," as she called them, but also from her short fiction. Her first book, *Enough Rope*, was a best seller, going through eleven printings in fifteen months. At one point she was so famous that people followed her around waiting for her to say something funny; even worse, complete strangers accosted her, begging for a joke. Luckily, she was often up to the task. A woman at a party asked if she was Dorothy Parker. "Yes, do you mind?" was her quick reply. In a 1956 interview with the *Paris Review*—the only serious literary question-and-answer session she ever sat for—Parker recalled, "Why, it got so bad that they began to laugh before I opened my mouth."

Much of Dorothy's humor relied on satire. Her keen eye for socially damning detail was evident in the very first poem she sold, a thirty-six-line piece she submitted to *Vanity Fair* in 1915, called "Any Porch." She was paid the sum of twelve dollars, more than a week's pay. The poem, with its rhyming iambic couplets of droll dialogue, provided New York with its first taste of Dorothy's ability to carefully observe and devastatingly mock the vapid inanities of the socialites who brushed up against her world. Here is an excerpt:

> *"I'm reading that new thing of Locke's—*
> *So whimsical, isn't he? Yes—"*
> *"My dear, have you seen those new smocks?*
> *They're nightgowns—no more, and no less."*
> *"I don't call Mrs. Brown bad,*
> *She's un-moral, dear, not immoral—"*
> *"Well really, it makes me so mad*
> *To think what I paid for that coral!"*
>
> *"My husband says, often, 'Elsie,*
> *You feel things too deeply, you do—'"*
> *"Yes, forty a month, if you please,*
> *Oh, servants impose on me, too."*

Dorothy drew inspiration from what she witnessed in her social and professional life. She mimicked the language she heard and lampooned her hosts and companions in brilliant stories and clever verse. She was one of the earliest contributors to *The New Yorker* and had much to do with its rise in prestige. Yet stories such as "Dialogue at Three in the Morning" and "Arrangement in Black and White" satirized the very readers the new magazine was cultivating.

A Place at the Table:
Dorothy Parker and the Vicious Circle

Though she skewered her friends and enemies, there were a few other New Yorkers with a sensibility akin to Dorothy's, and they soon found a common meeting ground. Just as one cannot think of mixing a proper

"What the Hell?"
Words and Phrases Attributed to Parker

"What the hell?" is just one of many phrases that Dorothy Parker is credited with popularizing, according to editor Stuart Y. Silverstein, who put together *Not Much Fun: The Lost Poems of Dorothy Parker* (Scribner) in 1996. Spending hundreds of hours poring over old copies of magazines and newspapers, he managed to dig up 122 pieces that Dottie had written and, for whatever reason, neglected to publish in her three books of collected verse. (One wag said that Dottie is sure to punch Silverstein in the nose when she meets him in heaven.)

Silverstein says that Parker made numerous contributions to everyday speech, although he also noted in an interview that "in virtually all instances the person credited with the first known use of a word or phrase almost certainly did not create it. . . . Most words emerge from a hazy mist—suddenly, there they are, out of nowhere."

According to Silverstein, the first *documented* use of the following words, terms, and phrases can be attributed to Dorothy Parker: art moderne, ball of fire (said of a person), with bells on, bellyacher, birdbrain, boy-meets-girl, chocolate bar, daisy chain (in the sexual sense), face-lift, high society, mess around (to potter), nostalgic, one-night stand (in the sexual sense), pain in the neck (said of a person), pass (sexual overture), doesn't have a prayer, queer (gay), scaredy-cat, shoot (expletive), the sky's the limit, to twist someone's arm, what the hell, and wisecrack.

martini without dry vermouth, Dorothy Parker's story cannot be served without acknowledging her membership in the Algonquin Round Table. This gathering of misfits and cutups—writers, press agents, actors, and hangers-on—wrote itself into American popular culture in the twenties by living the Jazz Age lifestyle and reporting that life to their audiences. They typified, for many, a Manhattan of late nights in theaters, early mornings at house parties and speakeasies, long lunches, and a small bit of work squeezed in somewhere.

The group started meeting in June 1919, when the Algonquin Hotel hosted a welcome-home luncheon roast in honor of Alexander Woollcott, the *New York Times* drama critic, recently returned from two years in France as an enlisted man in the Great War. Although Dorothy produced much of her finest and most enduring work during this manic decade, it was her connection to the Round Table that made her a popular cultural icon of the Jazz Age. The group was practically inseparable, and with so many newspaper writers among them, their comings and goings were reported in the daily columns. On many afternoons, Dottie might be the only female present, and her circle of friends could always count on her to say something wryly amusing.

You Might as Well Live

Beyond her daily lunches at the Algonquin Round Table, Dorothy Parker's private life was rocky and provided a seemingly endless source of material for her fiction, poems, screenplays, and plays. During the Round Table years, she had several breakups and reconciliations with her first husband, Eddie Parker. The estrangement caused by the recurring absence of Eddie (and, some twenty-five years later, her second husband, Alan Campbell) due to wartime service shows up in her 1943 short story "The Lovely Leave." The growing distance between Eddie and Dorothy, psychologically and physically, contributed to their divorce in 1928. Dorothy also had a string of love affairs, often ending in disaster. By the time she was forty, she had tried to take her own life at least three times, often as a result of her loneliness.

As Dorothy's many relationships foundered, she solidified a lifelong preoccupation with death. This fascination is perhaps understandable, since she had lost her mother, stepmother, father, and a favorite uncle all before she turned twenty-one. Throughout her adult life, death was never far from her thoughts. The very titles of her books hint at death (*Enough Rope, Sunset*

Dorothy and Alan in 1937 at the Newark airport, boarding a transcontinental flight back to Hollywood. The pair were making a fortune writing for the movies at the time and had just bought a home in Bucks County, Pennsylvania.

Gun, Death and Taxes, Laments for the Living), and images of death and burial appear repeatedly in her work. She even subscribed to undertakers' trade journals while working at Vanity Fair and wore tuberose, a perfume favored for dressing corpses.

Romantic misadventures and the ongoing flirtation with suicide that they inspired accentuated her sense of death's omnipresence. When she wrote her O. Henry Award–winning short story "Big Blonde" in 1928, she had already attempted suicide twice. This may explain why Hazel Morse, the tragic protagonist of the story, reflects, "The thought of death came and stayed with her and lent her a sort of drowsy cheer. It would be nice, nice and restful, to be dead." For Parker, life was not sacred and untouchable, as she commented in 1928's "Coda":

> There's little in taking or giving,
>   There's little in water or wine;
> This living, this living, this living
>   Was never a project of mine.
> Oh, hard is the struggle, and sparse is
>   The gain of the one at the top,
> For art is a form of catharsis,
>   And love is a permanent flop,
> And work is the province of cattle,
>   And rest's for a clam in a shell,
> So I'm thinking of throwing the battle—
>   Would you kindly direct me to hell?

Dorothy's best defense against the darkness and sadness pervading her life was to attack; she built her reputation by using humor to defuse heartache and loneliness as much as to skewer social pretensions and emotional shallowness. For example, in "Autumn Valentine" (1935), Parker twists the standard trope of a broken heart to illustrate how ephemeral even "true love" can actually be:

> In May my heart was breaking—
> Oh, wide the wound, and deep!
> And bitter it beat at waking,
> And sore it split in sleep.
>
> And when it came November,
> I sought my heart, and sighed,
> "Poor thing, do you remember?"
> "What heart was that?" it cried.

She could not afford to be all doom and gloom, however; Dorothy was a freelance writer dependent on publishing in general-interest magazines, and her editors paid her to amuse and entertain. Even though she completed less than eight years of formal education, quitting school at fourteen, she got by well enough to write for a pantheon of the best American magazines, including Vogue, Vanity Fair, and The New Yorker, because she could amuse and entertain with the best of them. Her first job, working at Vogue for Condé Nast, paid her ten dollars a week. In her spare time she wrote and sold light verse. Her big break came when she joined Vanity Fair and started writing drama reviews. With her byline becoming more common, she branched out into short fiction, selling pieces to The New Yorker. Eventually she compiled her favorite pieces in single volumes, and those books quickly became best sellers. And when Hollywood came calling, she went west and started pulling in big checks to put words in the mouths of actors for the early talkies.

Her main audience throughout her career was women, and she got a lot of mileage—literally and figuratively —out of whom she called "the men I'm not married to." No one, though, was safe; she could turn just as easily against her readers themselves. Her subject might be the bore at the dinner party or the silly flapper on the street; she treated them all with a lacerating insight born of practiced cynicism. She particularly liked to adopt the air of the put-upon observer, such as in her "hate verse" about women:

> I hate Women;
> They get on my nerves.
> There are the Domestic ones.
> They are the worst.
> Every moment is packed with Happiness.
> They breathe deeply
> And walk with large strides, eternally hurrying
>   home
> To see about dinner.
> They are the kind
> Who say, with a tender smile, "Money's not
>   everything."
> They are always confronting me with dresses,
> Saying, "I made it myself."
> They read Woman's pages and try out the recipes.
> Oh, how I hate that kind of woman.

Parker wrote a series of these hate verses on such subjects as actors, men, her office, and wives, in which her powers of insight and observation sharpen her social commentary to a wicked-fine edge.

Halfway to the Door: Dorothy and Religion

In the early 1900s, with the wave of immigrants hitting American shores—and particularly the streets of New York—came a growing awareness of the role of Jewish life in a modern America. And yet, although Dorothy Parker's memorial plaque in Baltimore mentions her Jewish past, her identification with that heritage was uncommon. She was raised as a WASP. Her mother was Scottish; her father was Jewish but not observant, despite buying real estate among Jewish neighbors in West End and working in an industry—the garment trade—that had a long tradition with the religion. Dottie's father enrolled her in a West 79th Street Roman Catholic elementary school, concealing her Jewish roots from the nuns. Perhaps Henry was merely following the traditional understanding of Jewish identity: A Jew is someone who was born to a Jewish mother or who converts to Judaism in accordance with Jewish law and tradition. Yet when Dottie reminisced about her time at the convent school, she referred to herself as a "little Jewish girl trying to be cute"; thus, at some level, she could not conceal her heritage from herself.

From an early age Dorothy saw religion, something others took so seriously, as both a burden and a farce. Where others turned to religion for comfort, she thought of God as the one who took away her mother and replaced her with an evil stepmother. Dottie did not practice Judaism—or any religion, for that matter—at any time in her life. Her mother, stepmother, and both husbands were Christians, but her marriages were all civil ceremonies, and she claimed that one of the reasons she married Eddie Parker was for his "clean" surname, which she kept for the remainder of her life. While her stepmother, Eleanor, was fervently religious and demanded that young Dottie say prayers at bedtime, a belief in God could not have been easy for this girl who had experienced so much loss at such a young age. One wonders what the prayers of little Dorothy Rothschild were like.

We can see Dorothy's unusual take on religion in "Prayer for a New Mother" (1928). The surprisingly tender ballad imagines the loss Mary must have felt after the Crucifixion:

> The things she knew, let her forget again—
> The voices in the sky, the fear, the cold,
> The gaping shepherds, and the queer old men
> Piling their clumsy gifts of foreign gold.
>
> Let her have laughter with her little one;
> Teach her the endless, tuneless songs to sing,

Grant her her right to whisper to her son
The foolish names one dare not call a king.

Keep from her dreams the rumble of a crowd,
The smell of rough-cut wood, the trail of red,
The thick and chilly whiteness of the shroud
That wraps the strange new body of the dead.

Ah, let her go, kind Lord, where mothers go
And boast his pretty words and ways, and plan
The proud and happy years that they shall know
Together, when her son is grown a man.

Although Parker certainly wasn't a regular at church or temple, her friends were aware of the mixed-religion no-man's-land of her childhood and teased her about it. When Aleck Woollcott taunted George S. Kaufman at the Round Table, bellowing, "You goddamn Christ killer," Kaufman defused the tension that his anti-Semitic friend had wrought by declaring with mock exaggeration, "For my part, I've had enough slurs on my race. I am now leaving this table, this dining room, this hotel, never to return." He paused to glance across the table at Mrs. Parker looking at him. He smiled back and said: "And I trust Mrs. Parker will walk out with me—halfway."

No One-Night Stand: Dorothy Parker's Legacy

On June 7, 1967, Dorothy Parker could finally put to rest her questions about the afterlife. She suffered a fatal heart attack in her apartment, with only her poodle for company. Her obituary was splashed on the front page of the *New York Times* the next day. Summing up her impact was *New Yorker* editor William Shawn's assessment that Parker's personal and literary style "were not only highly characteristic of the twenties,

Books Published during Parker's Lifetime

Dorothy Parker never wrote a novel or an autobiography. All of her books that came out during her lifetime were collections of pieces she wrote for periodicals, sometimes with unpublished poems included as well. The first books she published were collections of poetry; when she had written enough short stories, these, too, were collected. After her death, other editions appeared. *The Portable Dorothy Parker* has stayed continuously in print since 1944; in 2006 it was expanded and revised.

Collected Poetry
Enough Rope (1926)
Sunset Gun (1928)
Death and Taxes (1931)
Collected Poems: Not So Deep as a Well (1936)

Collected Fiction
Laments for the Living (1930)
After Such Pleasures (1933)
Here Lies: The Collected Stories of Dorothy Parker (1939)

Collected Prose and Poetry
The Portable Dorothy Parker (1944)

but also had an influence on the character of the twenties—at least that particular nonserious, insolemn sophisticated literary circle—she was an important part of New York City." And indeed, that assessment still stands today, with only one revision: She is an important part of New York City.

Since Parker's death in 1967, her poems and short fiction have been collected in handsome editions that sell steadily. Independent scholar and literary sleuth Stuart Y. Silverstein startled Parker fans in 1996 by publishing *Not Much Fun: The Lost Poems of Dorothy Parker* with Scribner. He uncovered more than 120 "lost" poems and brought them back in print; Silverstein turned up a few more in 2009. In 2006, Penguin Classics revised and expanded *The Portable Dorothy Parker* and commissioned a new jacket by the Canadian comic book artist Seth. Penguin published *Complete Stories* (2002), *Complete Poems* (2009), and the 1953 play *The Ladies of the Corridor* (2008). Parker's name appears in print on a weekly basis, her poems have been turned into songs and recorded, and her likeness has appeared onscreen. Her fans are everywhere. In 1999, a *New York Post* gossip columnist followed Lou Reed to a photography exhibit. The rocker mentioned that one of the portraits in the show resembled Dorothy Parker; a fellow attendee asked who he was talking about. "What's wrong with you?" Reed asked. "Don't you

Dorothy in April 1953. This photo was taken by Roy Schatt in the garden of his studio on East 33rd Street.

people read anymore? How could you not have heard of Dorothy Parker?"

Of all the Round Table members, Parker is the only one who has remained in print continuously since her lifetime—*The Portable Dorothy Parker* has been in bookshops since 1944, when she first compiled and arranged it. Part of the *Portable's* attraction lies in the relevance of the observations as well as in the immediacy of the physical settings. Parker wrote about 63rd Street; the brownstones on that block are still standing ninety years later. Parker frequented the Plymouth, the New Amsterdam, the Cort— all theaters that have shows running this weekend. Her subject matter—honeymooners, telephone conversations, cousins, parties—is just as relevant today as when Herbert Hoover was in the White House. "A Telephone Call" (1927), one of her most popular short stories, is included in countless modern anthologies. Nine decades after she wrote the story, it was successfully presented in an off-off-Broadway performance, using a mobile phone as the prop—without changing a word of dialogue.

Present-day visitors to the Algonquin Hotel ask the staff if they can check into Parker's old room and order her favorite cocktails, to try to relive her life among her coterie of friends. Everywhere one looks today, from the dim lights in the Algonquin's lounge to the blinking marquees of the theater

The Dorothy Parker Society unveiled this plaque at 310 West 80th Street, where Dorothy's father died in 1913.

district, Dorothy Parker's humor and insight still ring true.

She was a woman of paradoxes: the self-described "little Jewish girl" who was educated by Catholic nuns, a caustic and often relentless social critic who was touchingly fond of animals and rarely without a pet dog, the dinner guest whom everyone wanted to be seated next to yet who was often lonely. Her exciting and sometimes tragic life bounced her all around Manhattan, so that few places there escaped her keen eye and often brutally insightful pen.

Dorothy Parker has become inseparable from Gotham. The oldest Broadway theaters hosted her small frame in their aisle seats. From apartments and hotels to bars and theaters, from dog-walking parks to the offices of friends and colleagues, each place she wrote about helps complete the picture.

The following pages explore Dorothy Parker through the New York that she inhabited. *A Journey into Dorothy Parker's New York* examines where this native New Yorker lived and worked in an effort not just to understand Dorothy better but also to get a better sense of New York City. Each location described here affected her in some fundamental way. In some locations, the connection is direct and obvious; in others, the effect on our understanding of Dorothy is cumulative and subtle. But each place guided her career and her legacy and is thus certainly worth including on the journey.

Chapter 2

An Apprenticeship in Cynicism
A Comfortable, Tumultuous Childhood

Dorothy Rothschild grew up on the corner of West 72nd Street and Broadway. This 1896 photo shows the nine-story Hotel St. Andrew (demolished in 1937), the Colonial Club building (torn down in 2008), and Rutgers Presbyterian Church (built in 1888 and still standing). An IRT subway station opened at the intersection in 1904.

In the 1890s, the Jersey Shore beach community of West End was popular with well-off Jewish New Yorkers. Many stayed at "cottages" such as these on the Atlantic.

This marker in Long Branch designates the site of where the Rothschild beach house once stood. Dorothy was born in this house, where her mother would die a few years later.

Dorothy Parker was good at laughing off her Garden State roots, joking that because her parents got her back home to Manhattan before Labor Day, she could be considered a true New Yorker. For the first twenty-three years of her life, she lived on Manhattan's Upper West Side. Like many New York City children, she spent her childhood in apartments. Dorothy was the youngest of four children, and her parents needed the space that a brownstone could provide. The neighborhood was bordered by Central Park to the east and the Hudson River to the west, though within those bounds her father never stayed in one place for more than three or four years. She had lived in almost a dozen places by the time she was twenty. Most of the Rothschilds' apartments were between the West Sixties and the West Eighties, not far from Central Park, and in them Dorothy crafted her first sonnets for her father. She walked her beloved Boston terriers, Rags and Nogi, in Riverside Park and Central Park.

After briefly attending a finishing school in Morristown, New Jersey, she spent her teenage years taking care of her father and working odd jobs. Dottie played the wisecracker and smart aleck from a young age—as the baby in the family, she probably developed these attributes naturally, as a defense mechanism. The precocious child would soon show exceptionally early development and maturity, especially in mental aptitude. But she didn't often write about these early years and rarely talked about them. In an interview eleven years before her death, she said, "All those writers who write about their childhood! Gentle God, if I wrote about mine you wouldn't sit in the same room with me."

Until the mid-nineteenth century, most of Manhattan's residents lived on the southern end of the island, below 14th Street, but as the population swelled in size during the immigration boom, the city pushed north and the Upper West Side became desirable. Many second-generation immigrants took apartments in the new

Seashore Birthplace and Tribute

Dorothy Parker's birthplace of West End is a sleepy little village that is part of Long Branch in Monmouth County. It lies just sixty miles from Manhattan; in the 1890s it was reachable from New York by steam ferry and railroad. The Rothschilds' cottage, with a separate carriage house, was near the present-day 732 Ocean Avenue, across the street from the beach.

Like the neighboring beach communities of Elberon and Deal, West End was a small town that swelled in the summer. In the nineteenth century, West End and Long Branch were among the most desirable places for New Yorkers to spend the sweltering summers. Locals brag that seven U.S. presidents visited there, and President Ulysses S.

neighborhoods of brownstones and apartment houses going up west of Central Park. Dottie's parents, Henry and Eliza, though not rich, were sufficiently well off to join the upper middle class there. Here on the West Side was where New York's first subway, August Belmont's Interborough Rapid Transit, opened when Dottie was nine. By cutting the commuting time between downtown and the new uptown neighborhoods, the subway made possible the construction of spectacular apartment buildings such as the Dakota, the Ansonia, and the Dorilton. In the middle of it all was "the Boulevard"—now Broadway—with landscaped trees and streetcar tracks.

A Developing Wit

The cynicism and mordant wit that were the hallmarks of Parker's career did not appear suddenly with her first job at *Vogue*; they were the product of a tumultuous childhood. On one hand, Parker led a comfortable life as a young girl, summering on the Jersey shore and at Long Island resorts, attending Broadway shows, and

The street where Dorothy grew up, Broadway, looking south from West 72nd Street, in 1897. Dorothy spent her entire childhood on the Upper West Side.

Grant's "summer White House" is a source of pride. The streets are lined with stately Victorians that have survived into the twenty-first century, contrasting with the numerous plain-looking condominiums that have been erected more recently along the water. Unlike Newport, Rhode Island, or Long Island's "Gold Coast," both of which drew mostly WASPs, the Jersey Shore drew many upper-class Jewish families. Among those were the Seligmans, a prominent banking family, and the Guggenheims, the Rothschilds' next-door neighbors.

Although Dorothy's birth was a happy event in West End, the village would forever be tinged with sadness for the family. A month shy of young Dottie's fifth birthday, her mother died at the house of coronary artery disease. Although it is not clear whether the Rothschilds ever returned to West End after Eliza's death, records show that the cottage burned down some years later. Henry held on to the property almost until his death.

More than a century after Dottie's birth, her birthplace was designated the first national literary landmark in the Garden State. In 2005, Friends of Libraries USA honored her with a marker in West End, a dedication cosponsored by the Dorothy Parker Society and the Long Branch Historical Association. A bronze plaque is attached to the entrance of the Fountain Apartments at 732 Ocean Avenue. Long Branch plays host to an annual Dorothy Parker Day, with events at the public library, community theater, and a cocktail lounge.

studying at one of the area's finest schools. On the other hand, her girlhood wasn't always pleasant: frequent deaths in the family, an evangelical step-mother bent on saving her Jewish soul for Jesus, and spent a lot of time with books rather than with playmates.

Despite having Jewish and Protestant parents, Dorothy attended a Roman Catholic convent school with her older sister, Helen. When she wasn't having run-ins with the nuns or with her step-mother, young Dottie was reading voraciously—a practice she later claimed was much better than a formal education. At eleven she devoured William Makepeace Thackeray's Victorian classic *Vanity Fair*, no doubt identifying with the novel's plain yet dangerously seductive protagonist, Rebecca Sharpe. Parker reminisced in 1956, "I read Vanity Fair about a dozen times a year. I was a woman of eleven when I first read it—the thrill of that line 'George Osborne lay dead with a bullet through his heart.'" In 1906, like almost every other girl in New York,

The Upper West Side in 1884, when it was first being developed, less than ten years before the Rothschilds moved there. This is the north side of West 73rd between Columbus and Central Park West, just a couple of blocks from where Dorothy would soon live.

Dottie was crazy about the stage sensation *Peter Pan* and its star, Maude Adams, and collected her photos. She also was a devoted fan of *St. Nicholas* magazine for children, filled with poetry, stories, cartoons, and humor. Generations of American children grew up reading short fiction and poetry interspersed with cartoons from this periodical—it was almost like *The New Yorker* for the junior set.

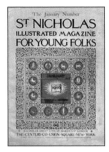

St. Nicholas magazine was published from 1873 until 1940 and featured the work of some of the best writers from Britain and America, including Mark Twain, Louisa May Alcott, Robert Louis Stevenson, Rudyard Kipling, and L. Frank Baum.

In the end, literature provided a literal escape as well. In 1914 the twenty-one-year-old Dottie submitted "Any Porch" to *Vanity Fair*, and it was accepted. This led to a junior staff position with the Condé Nast publishing company and enabled her to take a room at an uptown boardinghouse. While working for *Vogue* and *Vanity Fair*, Dottie commuted via the new underground Interborough Rapid Transit, or IRT. She submitted some poems to magazines and newspapers under her given name, Dorothy Rothschild, but sent others under made-up names such as "Henriette Rousseau" and "Helen Wells." She set many of her most famous stories and poems in her neighborhood, the Upper West Side.

This neighborhood, dominated by block after block of large apartment houses interspersed with wonderful four- and five-story brownstones and magnificent beaux arts

buildings, is essentially unchanged since Parker lived there decades ago. In her day it was becoming a haven for the upper middle class, whose lifestyle she portrayed in much of her work. Short stories such as "The Waltz" and "The Garter" are set at parties that appear to be

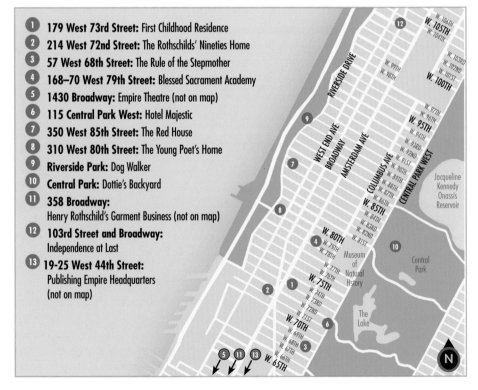

1. **179 West 73rd Street:** First Childhood Residence
2. **214 West 72nd Street:** The Rothschilds' Nineties Home
3. **57 West 68th Street:** The Rule of the Stepmother
4. **168–70 West 79th Street:** Blessed Sacrament Academy
5. **1430 Broadway:** Empire Theatre (not on map)
6. **115 Central Park West:** Hotel Majestic
7. **350 West 85th Street:** The Red House
8. **310 West 80th Street:** The Young Poet's Home
9. **Riverside Park:** Dog Walker
10. **Central Park:** Dottie's Backyard
11. **358 Broadway:** Henry Rothschild's Garment Business (not on map)
12. **103rd Street and Broadway:** Independence at Last
13. **19-25 West 44th Street:** Publishing Empire Headquarters (not on map)

taking place in the neighborhood. Her short story "Sentiment," published in May 1933 in *Harper's Bazaar*, is set inside a taxicab hurrying down these very streets:

> And then there's the doctor's house, and the three thin gray houses and then—oh, God, we must be at our house now! Our house, though we had only the top floor. And I loved the long, dark stairs, because he climbed them every evening. And our little prim pink curtains at the windows, and the boxes of geraniums that always grew for me. And the little stiff entry and the funny mail-box, and his ring at the bell. . . . I will see our tree and our house again, and then my heart will burst and I will be dead. I will look, I will look.

Dorothy Comes Home

Henry and Eliza Rothschild weren't expecting their family's new addition to be born while they were still at their summer cottage in West End, New Jersey. Eliza, a frail woman in her forties, was seven months pregnant, and Henry thought the sea air would do her good. Years later Dorothy quipped, "That was the last time I was early for anything."

When Eliza was well enough to travel, mother and baby were brought home to ❶ 179 West 73rd Street, a few steps east of Amsterdam Avenue. According to the city directory, the family had been living here since at least 1892. Her father was listed as a cloak maker. When Dorothy was a baby, this was a beautiful area of handsome brownstones with front stoops, awnings, and tree-lined streets. Overhead were strung the wires of the New York Telephone Company, created in 1895 to serve 15,000 subscribers with simple four-digit numbers. Streetcars ran up the wide avenues, though horse-drawn hansom cabs were still a common sight on the

streets. Although many of the other brownstones from the era have survived to this day, the Rothschilds' building was demolished for a large apartment building sometime before World War II.

The Rothschilds' Nineties Home

When Dorothy Rothschild was still an infant, her parents moved the family to ❷ 214 West 72nd Street, a few doors down from Broadway, then called simply the Boulevard.

The 1890s building at 214 West 72nd Street is scheduled for demolition.

The corner of Broadway and West 72nd Street figured prominently in the first two decades of Dorothy's life. In this 1912 photo, the 1906 sculpture of composer Giuseppe Verdi is almost new. This area was transformed by the addition of a subway station in 2003.

All the apartments Henry bought or rented were near the 72nd Street address. At the time, rents in New York were reasonable, with new apartments being built at a rapid pace. Landlords seeking well-off, reliable tenants like the Rothschilds offered incentives to move in, which likely accounted for many of the family's frequent relocations. When baby Dottie lived in the 72nd Street brownstone, the building had awnings, a garden, a front stoop, and a private entrance; her parents and older siblings, Harold, Bertram, and Helen, occupied several rooms. Dottie probably lived there until her mother passed away at forty-seven, just shy of the child's fifth birthday.

Approval was granted by the local community board in 2012 to demolish the site and replace it with a much larger apartment house. The neighborhood remains one of the most desirable in all of New York, with some of the finest schools, best restaurants, and most fashionable homes. When it came time to find another apartment, Henry didn't look too far: West 68th Street was just around the corner.

Not Easy Being a Stepdaughter

At the turn of the century, Henry moved the family from West 72nd Street to a limestone row house at ❸ **57 West 68th Street.** He also remarried, to schoolteacher Eleanor Frances Lewis. The rather hasty remarriage to a Sunday school spinster didn't sit well with his children, especially his youngest daughter. Dottie disliked this woman who barged into her life when she was only six years old, resenting her role as a replacement for her mother. She hated being forced to say prayers before she went to bed, and was loath to call the woman "Mother" or any similar term.

"She was crazy with religion," Dottie confided to her friend Wyatt Cooper in the 1960s. "I'd come in from school; she'd greet me with 'Did you love Jesus today?' Now, how do you answer that? She was hurt because the older ones called her 'Mrs. Rothschild.' What else? That was her name. I didn't call her anything. 'Hey, you' was about the best I could do." Maybe Dottie was praying hard for something else: Eleanor died before the little girl turned ten.

On those rare occasions when Parker spoke of her childhood, she liked to make it appear that she had grown up in a Dickensian household. But she told at least one story that points to the loneliness of being the youngest in the family by almost ten years. One of her brothers was walking down the street with a pal, and they passed Dorothy. When the friend asked him if she was his little sister, he casually replied no, within earshot of the child, and they kept walking without a backward glance.

The family's nondescript row house still stands between Columbus Avenue and Central Park West. On the block are the same classic brownstones, the synagogue, and the Second Church of Christ, Scientist that Dorothy would have been familiar with as a girl. The block is also the former home of James Dean, who moved to 19 West 68th Street (a fifth-floor walkup) in the spring of 1953; Roy Schatt's iconic photo of Dean walking down a car-lined street was taken here. These days it is still a quiet residential block, much as it was when Dottie was a young girl walking to school at the Blessed Sacrament Academy or to Central Park with her constant companions, her dogs.

The Nuns and the Little Jewish Girl

The ❹ **Blessed Sacrament Academy** at **168–70 West 79th Street,** between Amsterdam and Columbus avenues, is still standing. This is where, as a young girl,

Young Dottie's school still stands on West 79th Street.

Dorothy Rothschild first honed the wit and talent that would make her famous. "Convents do the same things progressive schools do, only they don't know it," Parker told the *Paris Review* in 1956. "They don't teach you how to read; you have to find out for yourself. At my convent we did have a textbook, one that devoted a page and a half to Adelaide Anne Procter; but we couldn't read Dickens; he was vulgar, you know."

Dorothy and Helen, with a nine-year age difference, were both students at Blessed Sacrament. Parker told interviewers late in life that she had loathed the place, and joked that the school was chosen only because she wouldn't have to cross any major avenues to get there. To get her in, her father had claimed that she was Episcopalian, but Dorothy couldn't quite pull that off and often felt both isolated and out of place. By all accounts, she drove the Sisters of Charity crazy. It's easy to imagine that Dorothy's technique of muttering one-liners under her breath was perfected in the halls of Blessed Sacrament. Today the double brownstone still looks much the same, and it remains a school, though

not a Catholic one. In a stroke of irony that even Dorothy would enjoy, the current tenants are Rabbi Gunter Hirschberg Elementary School and Rodeph Sholom Nursery School.

A Young Fan of *Peter Pan*

When James M. Barrie's *Peter Pan* debuted in America at the ❺ **Empire Theatre, 1430 Broadway** (between 40th and 41st), in November 1905, twelve-year-old Dorothy Rothschild was among the young girls who contributed to its instant success. She was close to her sister, Helen, so perhaps they took in the show together. Girls at the time tried to outdo one another in repeat attendances of the show, which starred Maude Adams as Peter. Sitting in the audience with crisp white handkerchiefs, they waved furiously to show that yes, they did believe in fairies.

Dottie's 1906 postcard to her father asking for pictures of the star of *Peter Pan*.

Peter Pan ran from 1905 to 1907 at the Empire Theatre with Adams, and she returned to the role there in 1912 and 1915. While on vacation in Bellport, Long Island, in June 1906, young Dottie implored her father in a note, "If you see any pictures of Maude Adams, please send them to me." This early exposure to the magic of Broadway likely gave her a taste for the

Dorothy rode the Long Island Railroad from Pennsylvania Station to summer resorts. The beautiful building was demolished in the 1960s.

Uncle Martin on the *Titanic:*
Former White Star Lines Dock
Pier 54 (West Street at West 13th Street)

The sinking of the RMS *Titanic* in 1912 had a huge impact on Dorothy Parker, who lost her uncle in the tragedy. Like his brother, Martin Rothschild was an executive in the garment business; their parents, Samson and Mary, were German immigrants who had settled in Alabama in the 1840s.

Martin and his wife, Elizabeth Jane Barrett Rothschild, lived just nine blocks from Dorothy and her father, at 753 West End Avenue. (The home is gone, replaced by an apartment building.) The couple had no children. Henry was very close to Martin; Henry gave the Long Branch house where Dorothy's mother, Eliza, died to his brother.

Martin and Elizabeth were first-class passengers on board the *Titanic.* According to the *Encyclopedia Titanica,* after the ship hit the iceberg on the night of April 15, 1912, Elizabeth got into lifeboat no. 6 with twenty-two others while Martin stayed aboard the doomed ship:

> After the collision steward Frederick Dent Ray saw Mr. Rothschild coming out of his stateroom on C deck. "I spoke to him and asked him where his wife was. He said she had gone off in a boat. I said, 'This is rather serious.' He said, 'I don't think there's any occasion for it.'" Then the two men casually walked up to A deck where Ray went to a lifeboat.

Grief-stricken family and friends gather at Pier 54 as survivors from the tragic accident arrive in April 1912.

It's not known if Dorothy and Henry met Elizabeth and the other survivors when the *Carpathia* docked at Pier 54 on April 18, 1912. Martin's widow erected a memorial to him in the mausoleum where she herself was later interred at St. Mary's Cemetery, in Watkins Glen, New York. Dorothy, who mentioned her family members only briefly in her work, never wrote about the *Titanic*. She was certainly not adverse to passenger ships, and sailed to Europe several times.

Today the old Pier 54 is part of Hudson River Park and steamships are just a memory. The old sign is still faintly visible in the rust, WHITE STAR LINES barely legible.

---

critic's life; a little more than ten years later she was back at the same theater as a reviewer. The theater was demolished in 1953; now an office building stands at the same location.

Coming of Age in New York

The years of Dorothy's childhood travails—from the death of her stepmother through her return from boarding school and the time immediately afterward—

are sketchy at best. She spent summers with her sister at resorts on Long Island, but she wrote little. More than likely, most of her time was spent in the company of her father, whose health was deteriorating. Henry moved the two of them to several different apartment houses on the Upper West Side; all the homes were near each other and the park.

As a teenager, her schooling behind her, Dorothy was living with her now twice-widowed father in the

❻ Hotel Majestic, 115 Central Park West. Dorothy lived in the luxury residential hotel with her father briefly after the death of her stepmother. The Majestic was known as "the Jewish place" for having less restrictive social policies than other hotels; this suited the assimilation desires of Henry Rothschild. Directly across the street was another landmark apartment house, the Dakota, which opened in 1884.

The Majestic was built in 1894 by Albert Zucker. Twelve stories tall, it had private bowling alleys, a grand lobby, horse-drawn carriages out front, and a rooftop garden. With its six hundred rooms, it was one of the best places to live in the city, and being there gave young Dorothy a chance to observe

Opened in 1894 and demolished thirty-five years later, the Hotel Majestic was replaced by apartments carrying the same name.

firsthand many of the well-to-do people who would later resurface in her fiction and poetry. Her story "An Apartment House Anthology," published in the *Saturday Evening Post* of August 20, 1921, could easily be set in the Majestic:

> *What is really the keynote of the Tippetts' living room is the copy of the Social Register lying temptingly open on the table. It is as if Mrs. Tippett had been absorbed in it, and had only torn herself from its fascinating pages in order to welcome you. It is almost impossible for you to overlook the volume, but if you happen to, Mrs. Tippett will help you out by pointing to it with an apologetic little laugh. No one knows better than she, she says, that its orange-and-black binding is all out of touch with the color scheme of the room; but, you see, she uses it for a telephone book and she is simply lost without it. Just what Mrs. Tippett does when she wants to look up the telephone number of her laundress or her grocer is not explained.*

The Majestic currently at 115 Central Park West is not the same building that Dottie resided in as a teenager. The Hotel Majestic was demolished at the end of the 1920s, and the current art deco building on the site opened in 1931. Its two towers, designed by Irwin S. Chanin and Jacques Delamarre, are distinctive West Side landmarks that rise thirty-two stories. Note the Art Deco style and distinctive corner window's steel cage design. Round Table members Edna Ferber and George and Beatrice Kaufman also made their homes at the Majestic.

The Red House

The family hopped from one apartment to the next, always looking for better rents and a fresh start. They found a good deal on the West Side, only five blocks

· RED · HOVSE ·

350 West 85th Streeet, the Red House.

away, in an even more spectacular apartment house at ❼ **350 West 85th Street,** a luxurious six-story red-brick building between West End Avenue and Riverside Drive. Named "the Red House," it was designed and built by Harde and Short in 1904 and today is a city landmark. It has a combination of French neo-Gothic and Renaissance elements. It was built at a time when apartments were replacing row houses as the Upper West Side's dominant type of residence.

The Red House, which resembles an Elizabethan manor, is practically across the street from Riverside Park and its views of the Hudson River. It would have been a convenient spot for someone with a household of dogs, providing an easy base from which to walk them. This girlhood home of Dorothy's is almost directly across the street from the 1920s home of Heywood Broun and Ruth Hale, at 333 West 85th Street. Many legendary parties were held in the Broun-Hale home, which Heywood had won in a high-stakes poker game. (Fittingly, he later lost it at the card table.)

A Young Poet

Around 1900, the family had moved again, this time to a beautiful six-story limestone apartment house at ❽ **310 West 80th Street,** between West End Avenue and Riverside Drive. Dorothy's older brothers and sister soon moved to homes of their own, however, leaving the teenager alone to care for her father. Henry

27

was not well, suffering from the failing heart that would eventually kill him. As with Dorothy, death was also at the forefront of Henry's mind; he had already lost two wives, his younger brother, and both parents. Now it was just Henry, Dorothy, and the dogs.

The Civil War Monument in Riverside Park, a dog walker's destination.

Young Dorothy penned early pieces of light verse during this time. Only scraps survive, from postcards and letters sent to her father. He wrote back to her, always in sonnets and ballads. In that row house, getting older, deciding what she wanted to do with her life, she quite possibly dreamed of becoming a professional writer. In the summer of 1905, around the time she was living at this address, she sent a letter to her father from Bellport, Long Island:

> *I am having a lot of fun,*
> *Tho' my neck and arms*
> *Are burned by the sun.*
>
> *Doesn't "tho" look poetic?*
> *—Dorothy*

On December 27, 1913, Henry Rothschild suffered a fatal heart attack. Dottie would tell people she was now an orphan (although she was twenty years old). She liked generating sympathy, and being a young woman without parents got her the attention she craved.

Girlhood Walk

Visitors to New York who think that the only park in Manhattan is Central Park are missing out on a special place. ❾ **Riverside Park** is a narrow, 266-acre stretch of land squeezed between the Hudson River and Riverside Drive. It was planned and laid out by Frederick Law Olmsted, the architect who cocreated Central Park. Young Dorothy Rothschild came here on family outings to the Soldiers' and Sailors' Monument, located at 89th Street and Riverside Drive. A family photo shows her holding her dogs in front of the monument.

When Dorothy was young, the monument, with its marble sculpture and graceful terraces, was brand-new. It was completed in 1902, at a time when nostalgia for the Civil War was high. The cylindrical building is an

Central Park, green and serene.

enlarged version of the Hellenistic Monument of Lysicrates in Athens. The names of the military leaders Sherman and Farragut are inscribed there, along with such battle sites as Gettysburg, Vicksburg, and Antietam.

This is a lovely, quiet place to bring a book. The twenty-minute walk from Riverside Park to Central Park is one of the most enjoyable strolls in Manhattan.

Dottie's Backyard

Except for the years she would later spend in California and Pennsylvania, Dorothy spent her entire life within a few blocks of ⑩ Central Park. But as a child, she wasn't much interested in skipping rope, and she had few friends. More likely Dottie found the park a peaceful place to walk her dogs, just as residents still do a century later. In a city of paved streets, it is the woodsy backyard for more than 1.5 million Manhattan residents, and more than 25 million people visit it each year. When she wasn't walking her dog in the park, Dorothy likely walked with her sister Helen. But they didn't frolic on play structures; playgrounds were not popular in Central Park in the early twentieth century, and the wealthy residents of apartment buildings bordering the park fought the city to prevent their installation. The first playgrounds in the park were built in 1934.

The Life of Reilly

Dorothy Parker's love of animals, especially dogs and horses, is well documented. She was almost never without a pet dog. In July 1921 she published "To My Dog" in *Life*. It could just as well have been written about a man as about man's best friend:

I often wonder why on earth
You rate yourself so highly;
A shameless parasite, from birth
You've lived the life of Reilly.
No claims to fame distinguish you;
Your talents are not many;
You're constantly unfaithful to
Your better self—if any.
Yet you believe, with faith profound,
The world revolves around you;
May I point out, it staggered 'round
For centuries without you?

Cartoons and Canines

One of Dorothy Parker's favorite people was *The New Yorker's* James Thurber. A writer, cartoonist, and humorist, Thurber shared Parker's love of animals. She wrote the introduction to his best-selling collection of cartoons, *Men, Women and Dogs* (1943). "I have always found it best to be quiet and alone with a Thurber drawing," she wrote, "that I may seek to fathom what went on in the lives of the characters depicted, before the artist chose his moment for setting them down forever. Sometimes I wonder if eternity is going to be half long enough for me to make anything near a reasonable guess."

James Thurber.

Parker particularly loved strays and once rescued one late at night on Sixth Avenue. She took the pooch home, cleaned it up, and presented it to affluent friends on Long Island. The thought of a mutt living in such rich digs amused her. She had dogs as companions throughout her life, no matter where she was living. She even signed telegrams to friends and family as if from her pooch. When she sat for portraits, she liked having a dog for company. And when she passed away in 1967, she was living alone with a poodle.

Horses also frequent Dorothy's writing; she may have grown up a city girl, but horses were a big part of her daily life. After a night on the town, Dorothy was known to stop and admire hansom cabs. Her short story "Just a Little One," published by *The New Yorker* in May 1928, conveys her feelings:

> *Don't let me take any horses home with me. It doesn't matter so much about stray dogs and kittens, but elevator boys get awfully stuffy when you try to bring in a horse. You might just as well know that about me now, Fred. You can always tell that the crash is coming when I start getting tender about Our Dumb Friends. Three highballs, and I think I'm St. Francis of Assisi.*

By the end of the story, she wants to "go out and get a horsie."

The Garment Business

Henry Rothschild ran a thriving men's cloak business at ⑪ **358 Broadway**, between Franklin and Leonard streets, when daughter Dorothy was born in 1893. Biographer Leslie Frewin says he was "a fairly prosperous cloak and suiter" employing more than two hundred employees in the booming garment district. A merchandising pioneer in the wholesale cloak and suit trade, he was among the most prosperous garment industry executives of the era, doing well enough to be admitted to exclusive associations such as the Progress and Criterion clubs.

The 1893 New York City Directory lists 358 Broadway as Rothschild's business. It was probably an office or showroom, with workers in other buildings (away from the public eye) sewing the merchandise. It is not known whether Mr. Rothschild used sweatshops full of women and children to make the garments for his firm; if not, he would have been a most remarkable exception, for this practice was all but universal at the time. New York City's sweatshops have a tragic history.

The 1911 Triangle Shirtwaist Factory fire, for instance, which claimed the lives of 146 workers, many of them immigrant girls, occurred at 23–29 Washington Place, at the northern corner of Washington Square East, a little over a mile from Rothschild's store.

Henry Rothschild was not completely unmindful of his workers, however. At Christmastime, he and Dorothy traveled in a horse-drawn coach to the Lower East Side, where many workers lived. She watched from the carriage while her father handed out neatly sealed envelopes of cash to those in need.

Henry's former business was located in what is now TriBeCa (the "Triangle Below Canal Street"), one of the hottest neighborhoods in the city. The warehouses and factories of the old garment businesses have been revamped into spacious loft apartments, and with the influx of luxury building conversions have come upscale shops, restaurants, and art galleries. In 2012, Henry's five-story building sold for almost $13 million.

Independence at Last

When Dorothy Rothschild sold her first poem, "Any Porch," in 1914, to Frank Crowninshield of *Vanity Fair*, her literary life began. After countless rejections from many of the best publications, the acceptance of the poem gave her the confidence to march down to the Condé Nast offices and seek a job. The gamble paid off; she was hired for ten dollars a week for light editorial work at *Vogue*, *Vanity Fair's* sister publication. With an entry-level publishing job secured, Dorothy took a room at a boardinghouse at ⓬103rd Street and Broadway, a building equidistant from her siblings' homes. (After her father died in 1913, she had lived with them off and on.) The IRT had recently opened a station at 103rd Street, and apartments were being built nearby. She was happy in the boardinghouse and made friends there, among them Thorne Smith, an

advertising copywriter who would later create *Topper*, the popular comedy about mischievous ghosts.

The neighborhood hasn't changed much in a century, and the corner of 103rd and Broadway today is very similar to what it was like in 1914. It is still residential with a wide mix of social classes sandwiched between Riverside Park on the west side and Central Park on the eastern border. The exact building occupied by the twenty-one-year-old remains a mystery, however; they all look alike. While living at 103rd and Broadway, Dorothy launched her professional career. This was also where she started seeing a rakish stockbroker at Paine, Webber & Company, Edwin Pond Parker II, whom she'd met at a summer resort. When the couple married in 1917, Dorothy was working at *Vogue*, about to begin the most exciting chapter of her life.

From *Vogue* to *Vanity Fair*

The nondescript office building at ⓭19–25 West 44th Street was the home of the Condé Nast publishing empire before the First World War. Nast bought *Vogue* in 1909, when circulation was less than 23,000, and he made Edna Woolman Chase managing editor in 1914. That same year Dottie joined the staff, and she continued to work at Condé Nast until 1920— a period of remarkable growth under Chase's leadership. Dottie started off composing captions for fashion spreads in *Vogue*, doing the work of what today would be called an editorial assistant. Even at this early stage of her career, we see signs of the wit that was developing under her editor's nose. Among her captions were such dollops as "Brevity is the soul of lingerie—as the Petticoat said to the Chemise"; "This little pink dress will win you a beau"; and "Right Dress! For milady's motor jaunt."

Dottie was the staff guinea pig for hairstyle experiments and other fashion tests. The atmosphere was fairly

Dorothy Rothschild's first literary employers. "Any Porch" was accepted by editor Frank Crowninshield, left, at *Vanity Fair*'s West 44th Street office. He is sitting with publisher Condé Nast and the legendary *Vogue* editor Edna Woolman Chase. Dottie was given a minor editorial assistant position at *Vogue*; when she left the magazine four years later, it was for a job as drama critic at *Vanity Fair*.

19–25 West 44th Street, Parker's launching pad.

Victorian, and female staffers were decorous; they even wore gloves in the office. She also sent her work across the hallway to *Vanity Fair*, which published her poetry and prose. "The Picture Gallery" appeared in the December 1918 issue, under the heading "Oh, Look— I Can Do It, Too":

My life is like a picture gallery,
With narrow aisles wherein the spectators may walk.
The pictures themselves are hung to the best advantage;
So that the good ones draw immediate attention.
Now and then, one is so cleverly hung,

That, though it seems obtrusive,
It catches the most flattering light.
Even the daubs are shown so skillfully
That the shadows soften them into beauty.
My life is like a picture gallery,
With a few pictures turned discreetly to the wall.

After four years, Dottie tired of the white gloves and the daily office drudgery at *Vogue*. To her rescue came the "gentle and courtly" Frank Crowninshield, who made her an offer. She jumped at the opportunity to go over to *Vanity Fair*, which he had launched in 1913 for sophisticated readers. (The magazine had once published an entire article in French.) The girl who never made it past eighth grade was made a copy editor. When critic and "Jeeves" creator P. G. Wodehouse left the magazine in 1918 to focus on his writing career, Crowninshield took a chance and assigned the office wisecracker to replace him as drama critic. She was observant, clever, and fearless—perfect characteristics for the city's first female theater critic.

The highlight of Dorothy's tenure at Condé Nast came in 1919, the year Robert Benchley was hired as managing editor. Soon after, he brought on Robert E. Sherwood, a towering man and aspiring playwright from New Rochelle, New York. The trio hit it off immediately and had a grand time as office mates. Dorothy, Benchley, and Sherwood must have been an unforgettable sight walking to and from lunch each day on 44th Street: By all accounts Parker stood about four feet eleven inches,

In 1918, *Vanity Fair* was required reading for the rich and influential.

Benchley six feet, and Sherwood six feet seven. Parker joked about the head-turning impression they made together, saying that the little people from the Hippodrome's vaudeville shows nearby were attracted to Sherwood for his extreme height.

Condé Nast Publications (purchased in 1959 by Samuel Irving Newhouse, Sr.) remained in the Times Square area for more than a hundred years, publishing *Vogue*, *Vanity Fair*, *GQ*, *Glamour*, and (since buying it in 1985) *The New Yorker*. Condé Nast signed a twenty-five-year lease in 2011 to move to 1 World Trade Center in 2015.

Working for Condé Nast set Parker up for a professional life as a writer. It was here that she got her feet wet in the publishing world and made contacts with people she would be associated with for the rest of her life. Her office was just a two-minute walk from the Algonquin Hotel, no doubt contributing to the frequency of her lunches there. As the next chapter of Parker's life began, she was headed on a journey toward success.

Chapter 3

Drink and Dance and Laugh and Lie
The Vicious Circle and All That Jazz

This 2002 painting by Natalie Ascencios hangs in the Algonquin Hotel's Roundtable Room. From left standing: Benchley, FPA, Sherwood, Marx, Woollcott, Connelly, Ferber. Seated: Parker, Ross, Kaufman and Broun.

After marrying Edwin Pond Parker II in 1917, Dorothy Rothschild became Dorothy Parker, the name she used for the rest of her life. She had changed professionally, too. Her informal apprenticeship was over when Frank Crowninshield tapped her to fill P. G. Wodehouse's shoes as drama critic for *Vanity Fair*, making her New York City's first female drama critic—and certainly one of its most famous.

Her professional and social lives began to blend when she took on another role that would make her a household name: reigning wit of the Algonquin Round Table. This group, an eclectic collection of writers, editors, publicists, and actors, exchanged clever banter and social pronouncements over lunch each day at the Algonquin Hotel. Although the group is justly famous for its wisecracking luncheons, the friendships and alliances were solidified during evening rounds at the theater, various speakeasies, and weekend lawn parties on Long Island. Indeed, members of the Round Table supported one another professionally. For Dorothy, it was the perfect stage on which to hone her craft; surrounded by brutally quick wits, she knew she had to be quicker.

Less than ten years after the Round Table began, it silently faded into memory when the regulars suddenly found themselves taken up with new occupations and successes. Dottie was not even there to witness the end of the era. When the twenties ended with a crash and the Algonquin hosted its last Round Table lunch, she was in Europe on an extended journey, the guest of her friends Sara and Gerald Murphy as they nursed their young son through tuberculosis.

The Round Table, as well as the relentless, never-ending party of the twenties, proved to be a boon for Dorothy Parker as a writer: In six years she brought out three collections of poetry; published short fiction in such prestigious magazines as *The New Yorker*, *Vanity Fair*, *Harper's*, and *Life*; won the O. Henry Award for her short story "Big Blonde"; and collaborated on several theater works, including two revues put on by members of what came to be known as the Vicious Circle.

Unfortunately, Dorothy's personal life during this period was less triumphant. She suffered the collapse of one marriage, a string of bad relationships and worse breakups, an abortion, hospitalization for nervous exhaustion, and at least three suicide attempts. Although Dorothy left no definitive record of how these traumatic events affected her—no diaries or journals, few personal letters—many of the experiences made their way into her poetry and prose. For example, her feelings about Eddie's departure for the war are rehashed in "The Lovely Leave" (1943). A woman is painfully lonely while her husband is attending military training in a nearby state. When he returns home for a brief leave, however, the couple finds that he can't really return to their previous life—the draw of his new world is too powerful:

> *You have companionships no—no wife can ever give you. I suppose it's the sense of hurry, maybe, the consciousness of living on borrowed time, the—the knowledge of what you're all going into*

> *together that makes the comradeship of men in war so firm, so fast. But won't you please try to understand how I feel? Won't you understand that it comes out of bewilderment and disruption and— and being frightened, I guess?*

Parker might have been re-creating an argument she had had with either of her husbands—both left her at home while they went to army training, and both returned changed men.

Always Someone on Her Arm

After her marriage to Eddie fell apart in the early 1920s, Parker was not at a loss for lovers. Although often lonely even in the company of friends, she— much like her character Hazel Morse in "Big Blonde"—managed to find willing male companions in an extended circle of friends and acquaintances. She counted among her many boyfriends Seward Collins, her editor at *The Bookman*, who ditched her when he tired of her by taking extended trips to Palm Beach; and Charles MacArthur, a newspaperman, raconteur, and budding playwright who was also Robert Benchley's drinking buddy. Parker was madly in love with Charlie. Unfortunately, Charlie had other lovers, as well as a wife back home in Chicago, and the affair ended miserably with an abortion and Parker's attempted suicide.

Parker's choice of boyfriends did not improve with time. In 1931 she met John McClain, a clerk in a Wall Street brokerage house. He was a good-looking rake of twenty-seven who had played football for Brown, and Mrs. Parker, thirty-eight, liked the attention he gave her. They soon became an item. Both got what they wanted: She, fearful that her youth and popularity were declining precipitously, acquired a handsome boyfriend; he acquired attention from the press merely

Dorothy in the late 1920s.

The Algonquin Hotel opened in 1902, where a room with a bathroom cost $2 to $3 a day. A restaurant fire in February 1909 drove 350 guests out into the cold in their pajamas. When the Round Table started meeting at the Algonquin in June 1919, the hotel had already been home to many writers and Broadway stars, such as Lady Gregory, John Drew, and Ethel Barrymore.

by virtue of being the man on her arm. He also acquired a better career. Parker spoke to a friend at the *New York Sun*, who found a reporter's job for McClain. Assigned to write the shipping news, he eventually wrote a column about the comings and goings of steamship travelers, called "The Sun Deck."

Parker craved McClain's attention. When he wasn't visiting her room at the Algonquin, she would telephone him throughout the day and night. He was less enamored, and by most accounts, after using her to get in the society pages, he tossed her aside. Parker responded with a suicide attempt.

Parker and the Reporter

The *New York Sun* at 280 Broadway, where Parker pulled some strings to land a job for her boyfriend John McClain, gave its name to the building where it took up residence in 1916. Founded in 1833 by printer Benjamin H. Day, the *Sun* became famous for its legendary editor Charles A. Dana, an early proponent of journalistic integrity and balanced news.

A famous exchange took place in the pages of the *New York Sun* in September 1897. Virginia O'Hanlon, of 115 West 95th Street—just around the corner from where Dorothy was living—wrote to the paper: "Dear Editor, I am 8 years old. Some of my little friends say there is no Santa Claus. Papa says if you see it in The Sun, it's so. Please tell me the truth, is there a Santa Claus?" Editor Francis P. Church replied, "Yes, Virginia, there is a Santa Claus."

After the *Sun* moved here in 1916, two fixtures were attached to the exterior, one displaying the time and the other the temperature. (Don't trust them, though; they are infamous for never being accurate.) The newspaper, facing dire financial difficulties, ended its 116-year run on January 4, 1950. In 2002 the *Sun* was revived, but it folded several years later; it is now published online as nysun.com.

280 Broadway, the former home of a legendary newspaper.

Aging Disgracefully

As she hit her thirties, Dorothy found herself moving from one lover to another, seemingly unable—or perhaps unwilling—to build a stable relationship, constantly seeking new conquests to keep herself entertained. In a candid moment of self-awareness and premonition in June 1924, she penned this ballad:

Ballade at Thirty-Five

This, no song of an ingénue,
This, no ballad of innocence;
This, the rhyme of a lady who
Followed ever her natural bents.
This, a solo of sapience,
This, a chantey of sophistry,
This, the sum of experiments,
I loved them until they loved me.

Decked in garments of sable hue,
Daubed with ashes of myriad Lents,
Wearing shower bouquets of rue,
Walk I ever in penitence.
Oft I roam, as my heart repents,
Through God's acre of memory,
Marking stones, in my reverence,
"I loved them until they loved me."

Pictures pass me in long review,
Marching columns of dead events.
I was tender and, often, true;
Ever a prey to coincidence.
Always knew I the consequence;
Always saw what the end would be.
We're as Nature has made us, hence
I loved them until they loved me.

L'ENVOI

Princes, never I'd give offense,
Won't you think of me tenderly?
Here's my strength and my weakness, gents,
I loved them until they loved me.

Reign of the Round Table

Hotels make unusual locations for literary history, and hotels in New York with true artistic connections are scarce. The Shelton (now the Marriott East Side) was home to Georgia O'Keeffe and Alfred Stieglitz for a decade. Media tycoon William Randolph Hearst built the Warwick for his famous friends. The Plaza is home

Staring at the Ceiling
Relationships with Men

Dorothy Parker's relations with men were a rich vein that she mined for her writing. "Men don't like nobility in women," she noted. "Not any men. I suppose it is because the men like to have the copyrights on nobility—if there is going to be anything like that in a relationship." Dorothy was especially fond of handsome younger men, although she was also tempted by a few who were older. This is a partial list:

Thorne Smith, writer
Eddie Parker, stockbroker (first husband)
John Garrett, writer
Elmer Rice, playwright
Ring Lardner, writer
Charles MacArthur, writer
Deems Taylor, composer
Seward Collins, writer
F. Scott Fitzgerald, writer
Alan Campbell, actor/writer (second husband)
Ross Evans, writer

to fictional six-year-old Eloise. And the Chelsea housed Sherwood Anderson, Brendan Behan, William S. Burroughs, Thomas Wolfe, and scores of other writers. But nothing really happened at these hotels; guests just checked in and sometimes wrote.

❶ The Algonquin, at 59 West 44th Street, is a literary landmark for another reason: it was a haven for writers and their de facto clubhouse. When a group of rascals made it their lunch destination for a decade, it achieved fame on a whole new level as the locus of the city's first literary celebrity group. Among the group welcoming Aleck Woollcott back home from the war

one day in June 1919 were newspaper columnist Franklin P. Adams (known as FPA) and the future editor of *The New Yorker*, Harold Ross. Dottie, age twenty-five, was then the drama critic at *Vanity Fair*.

As a sergeant on the armed forces newspaper *Stars and Stripes*, Woollcott had befriended a roster of New Yorkers who were also in publishing. The paper's managing editor was journeyman reporter Harold Ross, the only private in Paris with his own business cards. FPA, New York's most popular columnist, was an army captain on the staff. Other future Vicious Circle members in Paris during the war were reporters

59 West 44th Street, nirvana for writers and editors.

Heywood Broun and Jane Grant and artist Neysa McMein.

Many of the Round Table members, including Adams and Broun, were among the most popular journalists of their era. Their fans devoured their pronouncements and quoted their judgments as gospel. Yet today they are virtually forgotten. Though they wrote enough to fill a bookshelf of volumes, nothing they penned has been in print for decades. But in Parker's time they were stars. Of the other Round Table members, only Robert Benchley, Harpo Marx, Robert E. Sherwood, Edna Ferber, and George S. Kaufman still shine, and that is probably because they were connected to the stage and screen and not just the printed page.

Parker was one of the few female members of the Vicious Circle. Jane Grant, the first female general assignment reporter at the *Times*, was married to Harold Ross; Ruth Hale, a Broadway press agent, was married to Heywood Broun; and editor Beatrice Kaufman would drop in on her husband, George. On Saturday afternoons Edna Ferber would

1. **59 West 44th Street:** The Algonquin Hotel
2. **Sixth Avenue and 44th Street:** The Hippodrome
3. **25 West 45th Street:** Original *New Yorker* Offices
4. **28 West 44th Street:** Longtime *New Yorker* Offices
5. **Fifth Avenue and Central Park South:** The Plaza Hotel
6. **61 West 48th Street:** Boni and Liveright
7. **42 West 49th Street:** Jack and Charlie's Speakeasy
8. **45 West 49th Street:** Tony Soma's Speakeasy
9. **21 West 52nd Street:** "21" Club
10. **1466 Broadway:** The Knickerbocker Hotel
11. **412 West 47th Street:** Home of Jane Grant, Harold Ross, and Aleck Woollcott
12. **West 71st Street:** Mr. and Mrs. Parker's First Apartment
13. **252 West 76th Street:** Separate Lives
14. **57 West 57th Street:** Another Try at Living Together
15. **41 East 70th Street:** Presbyterian Hospital
16. **28 East 63rd Street:** Lenox Hill Living
17. **444 East 52nd Street:** Starting a New Life

take a break from her typewriter, and Neysa McMein would put down her paintbrushes, to join the group in the Rose Room. Other members were fascinating women: Margaret Leech was a Vassar grad and magazine writer who went on to win two Pulitzer Prizes in history. Peggy Wood and Margalo Gillmore were native New Yorkers who starred on Broadway; their careers stretched into films and live television. It is Dottie who is remembered most for being a part of the group, and it is the things she said at the table that are the most famous (so famous, Kaufman once remarked, that everything funny he ever said would someday be attributed to her). For example, when an acquaintance informed her that President Calvin Coolidge had died, she asked, "How can they tell?"

Stuart Y. Silverstein, who edited *Not Much Fun: The Lost Poems of Dorothy Parker*, said in an interview that the legacy of the Round Table is timeless: "The term 'the Algonquin Round Table' still holds substantial

Dottie was close to newspaperman-turned-playwright Marc Connelly. When working on his groundbreaking production *The Green Pastures* in the late twenties, he turned to her for assistance. She helped him transcribe a scene about the Exodus, later telling Connelly that she cried while typing it. The show won the Pulitzer Prize in 1930.

Edna Ferber was one of the most successful Round Table members. Her short stories were collected into best sellers, her novels sold hundreds of thousands of copies, and she saw much of her work turned into hit musicals and movies. She was never close to Dorothy Parker; the two tolerated each other, but only barely.

Sharing politics and a taste for nightlife with Dottie was Heywood Broun, one of New York's greatest newspaper stars. Broun, who grew up around the corner from the Rothchilds, was a gifted writer, beloved raconteur, and local celebrity who later wrecked his health as a labor organizer. Today all of Broun's books are out of print, but they are well worth looking for in used bookshops.

cultural resonance; for example, during [a recent] television season, at least three sitcoms employed it as an ironic punch line to skewer characters who spoke badly or stupidly. Is there any other person, or institution, or event from the interwar period that could possibly be used by a mass-market medium as an implicitly understood cultural reference? I cannot think of any—not even Lindbergh, not anymore. Perhaps the stock market crash. Endurance is its own testament." The Algonquin Hotel, the home base for the group

Alexander Woollcott was one of Dottie's dearest friends. The Round Table began in 1919 during a welcome-home roast for him. "Hello, repulsive" was his standard greeting. A charmer, raconteur, and gadfly, he was one of the best-known celebrities in the pre–World War II era.

that ruled the New York literary landscape during Prohibition, is on the edge of the theater district. Friends would meet in the Rose Room for long, uproarious lunches. Some nights there would be a poker game upstairs. After Dorothy split from Eddie for a second time in 1924, she moved into a furnished second-floor suite at the Algonquin. (Her pal Robert Benchley also rented a room there for a brief time.) Dorothy returned again in 1932; this is where she made one of her suicide attempts, this time with sleeping pills. Legend has it that she tossed a drinking glass out the window to draw attention to her plight.

Even when she wasn't depressed, Dorothy wasn't exactly a good tenant, and management couldn't count on her to pay the bill. Around Christmas one year, a friend asked Dottie if she was going to hang up a holiday stocking in her room. "No, I'm going to hang up [manager] Frank Case instead" was the ready reply.

"The Gonk," designed by Goldwin Starrett, opened for business in 1902. It is on the same street as the historic New York Yacht Club (37 West 44th), the Harvard Club (27 West 44th), the Penn Club (30 West 44th), the Bar Association (42 West 44th), and, on the other side of Fifth Avenue, the Cornell Club (6 East 44th)—hence the street's nickname of "Club Row." But even before the Round Table gang showed up, the place had a literary past; H. L. Mencken had been a guest years before, attracted to the Algonquin's reputation as "the most comfortable hotel in America."

After the Round Table moved on, the Algonquin continued to attract actors and literati—Graham Greene, Noël Coward, Sir Laurence Olivier, and Peter O'Toole all called the Gonk their home away from home, and William Faulkner drafted his Nobel Prize acceptance speech in his suite there in 1950.

The hotel was owned and managed for almost fifty years by the consummate hotelier Frank Case. "The Algonquin Hotel . . . is not the whole of New York," Case wrote in his 1938 memoir, *Tales of a Wayward Inn.* "There are other spots of interest and some distinction. The Algonquin is only the heart from which goes out warmth and light sufficient to make these other places possible for human habitation."

Case was quick to recognize the potential in currying favor with so many famous writers and wits, and his customers repaid him with generous amounts of ink in the city's daily newspapers. It was Case's custom to offer popovers to the group; the free food kept them coming back. FPA was the first to mention the Round Table, in his "Conning Tower" column; Silverstein says it is the first printed mention he can find of the group's

The biggest stage to ever entertain Broadway was at the Hippodrome.

The Hippodrome: The World's Largest Playhouse

Dorothy Parker and her Vicious Circle pals lived and worked in the shadow of the massive ❷ Hippodrome Theatre, across the street from the Algonquin Hotel. Advertised as the largest theater in the world, it had a stage that could hold a thousand performers.

The Hippodrome opened on April 12, 1905, straddling the entire east side of Sixth Avenue between 43rd and 44th streets. It was built by the same men who developed Coney Island's Luna Park and boasted 5,200 seats, ranging in price from twenty-five cents to a dollar. By far the largest Broadway theater, it presented spectacular shows, vaudeville, and silent movies. The Shuberts brought in a band of Sioux, put them in war paint, and had them perform a ghost dance in 1906. The Hippodrome could hold a two-ring circus; one memorable show featured an 8,000-gallon glass water tank that held chorus girls dressed as fish. In 1918 illusionist Harry Houdini made a five-ton elephant named Jenny and her trainer disappear on the Hippodrome stage. The publicists for the theater during the twenties were Murdock Pemberton and John Peter Toohey, original members of the Round Table.

Both the Sixth Avenue elevated train and the theater were demolished in 1939. After the building was torn down, the site became a parking lot until 1952, when a garage and office building went up at 1120 Sixth Avenue. Today the office tower retains its Hippodrome name. Inside the office tower lobby is a jumbo-size image of the old theater, the only memento of the original building.

formation. After Case's death in 1946, the Algonquin changed hands several times. In the last twenty-five years, more than $50 million has been invested on renovations and improvements to the Algonquin Hotel by a succession of owners and management companies. The most impressive renovation occurred in 2012, when Cornerstone Real Estate Advisers shut the hotel down completely for five months. The owners replaced 110-year old plumbing, refurbished every room, and brought the building into the twenty-first century.

The hotel has embraced its literary connections: the building façade includes bronze plaques indicating its landmark status; guests find complimentary books and publisher's galleys for upcoming releases in their hotel rooms; author talks and media parties are a regular feature of life at the Algonquin.

To walk into the lobby is to step into a time warp; it is easy to imagine the ghosts strolling across the tiled black-and-white floor (no doubt peering curiously at the patrons seated in cushy armchairs, accessing the Internet on their devices). The Round Table Room is adorned with a painting of the Vicious Circle by Brooklyn artist Natalie Ascencios, unveiled in November 2002 on the occasion of the hotel's centennial.

Beyond the Round Table

Like the Transcendentalists of the nineteenth century, the Round Table spawned a number of projects and collaborations among its members. Some of these projects, such as the musical revue *No Sirree!* were undertaken with the full support of the Round Table. Other schemes, such as publisher Harold Ross's idea to

start a magazine geared toward well-to-do Manhattanites, did not garner the same support. In fact, when Ross pitched the idea to his Vicious Circle friends, few had much faith in its success and some even told Ross to his face that he'd fail. Nevertheless, he did manage to convince a few people to go along with his plan. Jane Grant urged her husband to hit up a poker-playing cohort, Raoul Fleischmann, heir to the

The spot where the round table once stood.

family baking fortune. Fleischmann kicked in $25,000 in seed money to launch *The New Yorker*, with Ross and Grant putting up the rest.

Although much of the initial work of creating the magazine was done in Ross and Grant's house in Hell's Kitchen, *The New Yorker's* official offices were located at ❸ 25 West 45th Street from 1925 to 1935. Dorothy Parker was among the "editorial board" of Vicious Circle members whom Ross told potential advertisers and investors he had lined up to work on the magazine; others included Broun, Connelly, Ferber, Kaufman, Woollcott, Rea Irvin, and playwright Laurence Stallings. Years later Ross admitted to feeling sheepish about the deception; though he used their names, he never expected much—if any—work from them.

The first issue of *The New Yorker* appeared on February 21, 1925. The magazine was not a big hit with the Round Table or the target audience and almost went under a few times. In the fierce New York magazine market, the new publication had to find its voice. One of Ross's early

policies was to not use bylines for contributors, which protected some of his more famous friends from catching heat from their editors for doing work for the upstart magazine. In addition, Ross couldn't pay well, so he doled out stock—worthless at the time but worth quite a bit a

Members of the Algonquin Round Table

The hotel on West 44th Street has drawn those from the nearby publishing and theater world for more than 110 years. Whenever a convenient location is needed for a bite to eat or a place to meet, the Gonk serves the purpose admirably—and has done so since Teddy Roosevelt was in the White House. Many of the regulars who turned up in the hotel starting in 1919 worked for daily afternoon or evening newspapers, which had one o'clock deadlines, making for a nice long afternoon in which to while away their time.

- Franklin P. Adams (1881–1960): Columnist at *New York Tribune* and *New York World;* wrote "Conning Tower" column.
- Robert Benchley (1889–1945): *Vanity Fair* managing editor, *Life* drama editor; humorist; actor in short films.
- Heywood Broun (1888–1939): Sportswriter at *New York Tribune,* columnist at *New York World;* author; helped found Newspaper Guild.
- Marc Connelly (1890–1980): Newspaperman turned playwright; cowrote plays with George S. Kaufman; won Pulitzer Prize for play *The Green Pastures.*
- Edna Ferber (1887–1968): Novelist and playwright; won Pulitzer for *So Big;* wrote *Show Boat, Oklahoma, Cimarron,* and *Giant.*
- Margalo Gillmore (1897–1986): Actress and "the baby of the Round Table"; starred in early Eugene O'Neill plays.
- Jane Grant (1892–1972): First female *New York Times* general assignment reporter; cofounded *The New Yorker* with Harold Ross.
- Ruth Hale (1887–1934): Broadway press agent; helped pass Nineteenth Amendment for women's rights; married Heywood Broun.

Franklin Pierce Adams, aka FPA, was one of Dorothy's close friends. When the Round Table began in 1919, he was the senior member at age thirty-eight. He printed some of Dottie's most enduring poems in the *New York World* on August 16, 1925. Under the heading "Some Beautiful Letters," the batch included "Social Note," "News Item," "Interview," "Comment," and "Résumé." Of FPA, Dottie said, "He raised me from a couplet."

decade or so later. In five years the circulation climbed to 101,746; ten years after launching, it was 127,450.

Dorothy wrote drama reviews for the first two issues and contributed poems—"Cassandra Drops into Verse" (February 28, 1925) and "Epitaph" (July 18, 1925)—at the height of her career. Parker's first *New Yorker* short story was a peek inside a speakeasy similar to Tony's—the 900-word "Dialogue at Three in the Morning," in the February 13, 1926, issue:

- Beatrice Kaufman (1894–1945): Publishing house editor. Married George in 1917. Harpo Marx called her "Lamb Girl."
- George S. Kaufman (1889–1961): Playwright; *New York Times* drama editor, producer, director, actor.
- Margaret Leech (1894–1974): Magazine writer, novelist, playwright. Won Pulitzer Prize for history in 1942 and 1960.
- Herman J. Mankiewicz (1897–1953): Press agent; early *New Yorker* drama critic; cowrote plays with Kaufman; produced Marx Brothers movies; cowrote *Citizen Kane.*
- Harpo Marx (1888–1964): Actor; comedian; musician; card player.
- Neysa McMein (1888–1949): Magazine cover illustrator; painter.
- Dorothy Parker (1893–1967): *Vanity Fair* drama critic; *New Yorker* critic; celebrated poet; short story writer; playwright; screenwriter.
- Brock Pemberton (1885–1950): Broadway producer and director.
- Murdock Pemberton (1888–1982): Press agent; first art critic for *The New Yorker.*
- Harold Ross (1892–1951): Founded *The New Yorker* with Jane Grant.
- Art Samuels (1889–1938): Editor of *Harper's Bazaar.*
- Robert E. Sherwood (1896–1955): *Vanity Fair* drama editor; *Life* editor; author; playwright who won four Pulitzer Prizes and Oscar for *The Best Years of Our Lives.*
- Laurence Stallings (1895–1968): Ex-reporter; editorial writer for *New York World;* collaborated with Maxwell Anderson on *What Price Glory?*
- Donald Ogden Stewart (1894–1980): Author; playwright; screenwriter; blacklisted and barred from United States; won Oscar for *The Philadelphia Story.*
- Frank Sullivan (1893–1976): Early *New Yorker* writer; humorist.
- Deems Taylor (1886–1966): Music critic turned populist composer; wrote libretto for *The King's Henchmen* with Edna St. Vincent Millay; narrator of Disney classic *Fantasia.*

- John Peter Toohey (1880–1946): Theater press agent for *Dinner at Eight, You Can't Take It with You, Of Mice and Men, The Man Who Came to Dinner.*
- David Wallace (1889–1955): Theater press agent.
- John V. A. Weaver (1893–1938): Poet; literary editor of the *Brooklyn Eagle;* married Peggy Wood.
- Peggy Wood (1892–1978): Actress in musical comedies and plays; early TV star.
- Alexander Woollcott (1887–1943): Drama critic for *New York Times* and *New York World;* CBS radio star as the Town Crier, model for Sheridan Whiteside in Kaufman and Hart's *The Man Who Came to Dinner.*

Associates at the Table

These notables dropped by the Gonk or another of the circle's numerous party spots every so often.

- Tallulah Bankhead (1903–1968): Broadway, film, and TV actress; TV guest; career took her to *Batman* as Black Widow; her greeting "Hello, dahling" is more popular than her films.
- Ethel Barrymore (1880–1959): One of the greatest stars of Broadway, made her debut in 1894; early Hollywood star; sister of actors John and Lionel.
- Ring Lardner (1885–1933): Newspaper columnist; sportswriter; author; short story writer; playwright.
- Alice Duer Miller (1864–1942): Author and writer who worked for women's rights; wrote *Are Women People?* for *New York Tribune.*
- Herbert Bayard Swope (1882–1958): Executive editor of *New York World.*

"Plain water in mine," said the woman in the petunia-colored hat. "Or never mind about the water. Hell with it. Just straight Scotch. What I care? Just straight. That's me. Never gave anybody any trouble in my life. All right, they can say what they like about me, but I know—I know—I never gave anybody any trouble in my life. You can tell them that from me, see? What I care?"

For the next five years *The New Yorker* was Dorothy's prime spot to place short fiction, and the pieces from this time are some of her best known today, including "Arrangement in Black and White" (1927), "Just a Little One" (1928), and "You Were Perfectly Fine" (1929). These stories helped define what would become a "*New Yorker* story": a few thousand words in length, urbane, clever, and keenly insightful. Although the magazine can boast contributors as diverse as J. D. Salinger, Vladimir Nabokov, Truman Capote, and E. Annie Proulx, a line can be traced from Parker's short fiction about Manhattan to later stories by James Thurber, John O'Hara, and John Cheever.

These stories have helped the magazine define New York in the minds of readers across the country. Parker, in particular, used her status as a New Yorker both as a badge of honor and to prove a humorous point. For example, in her short story "Soldiers of the Republic" (which may not have been fiction), she relates the story of a

The New Yorker was once housed at 25 West 45th Street.

The Hippodrome's colorful producer Charles B. Dillingham (left) and Harold Ross playing golf in Indiana in 1935.

passerby in war-torn Valencia chuckling at the funny American woman walking down the street in a big hat: "I lived in a state of puzzled pain as to why everybody on the streets laughed at me. It was not because 'West End Avenue' was writ across my face as if left there by a customs officer's chalked scrawl." One famous anecdote about Dorothy's early *New Yorker* stint is often repeated. Ross spotted her in a speakeasy in the middle of the day. When he asked her why she wasn't at the office, working on a promised piece, she replied, "Someone else was using the pencil."

The New Yorker operated at that building until it moved a block away to ❸ **28 West 44th Street,** an address it would keep for nearly sixty years. Ross moved the magazine there in 1935, ten years after founding it.

Although life was becoming more fast-paced and "modern," Ross stipulated in the building lease that the landlord must keep at least one attendant-operated elevator in service.

Dorothy's contributions to the magazine after 1935 dropped steeply. Ross, who stayed at the helm until his death in 1951, wanted only "funny" pieces from her, and she was tired of such writing. As she became more politically active, Parker turned away from writing fiction set in speakeasies and poems about unrequited love. After 1935 she wrote only thirteen more stories for publication, six of which appeared in *The New Yorker* (compared to twenty in 1925–35 for *The New Yorker* alone). These later works included "Soldiers of the Republic" (1938), which she wrote after witnessing the civil war in Spain with her second husband, Alan Campbell. "Song of the Shirt, 1941" (1947) is a classic, partially based on her own experiences on the home front of the Second World War:

> *Headquarters was, many said, the stiffest office of all the offices of all the war-relief organizations in the city. It was not a place where you dropped in and knitted. Knitting, once you have caught the hang of it, is agreeable work, a relaxation from what strains life may be putting upon you. When you knit, save when you are at those bits where you must count stitches, there is enough of your mind left over for you to take part in conversations, and for you to be receptive of news and generous with it. But at Headquarters they sewed. They did a particularly difficult and tedious form of sewing. They made those short, shirt-like coats, fastened in back with tape, that are put on patients in hospitals. Each garment must have two sleeves, and all the edges must be securely bound. The material was harsh to the touch and the smell, and impatient of the needle of the novice. Mrs. Martindale had*

> *made three and had another almost half done. She had thought that after the first one the others would be easier and quicker to manufacture. They had not been.*

Also working for *The New Yorker* in this building were E. B. White, James Thurber, E. J. Kahn, Joseph Mitchell, Pauline Kael, and an office boy named Truman Capote. After Harold Ross's death, the editor's position fell to the taciturn William Shawn. He accepted Dorothy's last three short stories for *The New Yorker* at this office: "I Live on Your Visits" (1955), "Lolita" (1955), and "The Banquet of Crow" (1957). A plaque on the building's exterior salutes longtime *New Yorker* contributors but doesn't mention Dorothy Parker.

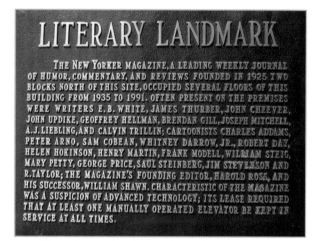

Legend has it that Brendan Gill wrote the text for this plaque affixed to 28 West 44th Street. Ross is the only Round Table member named on it.

In 1985 publisher S. I. Newhouse, Jr. bought control of *The New Yorker* for $168 million and added it to the roster of Condé Nast Publications. Newhouse instituted sweeping changes, and the staff moved out to join the company's other titles.

Dorothy Rothschild's first boss, editor Frank Crowninshield. She submitted "Any Porch" to him, and it was accepted and published in *Vanity Fair* in September 1915. He subsequently hired her to work for the magazine's sister publication, *Vogue*, as an assistant.

The Plaza Hotel shortly after it opened in 1907. Parker was fired from *Vanity Fair* here in 1920. Years later she returned as a guest of the hotel.

Pink Slip in the Palm Court

The ❺ **Plaza,** at **Fifth Avenue and Central Park South,** is a New York landmark with a distinct place in city history as the grandest hotel facing Central Park. It is also where Dorothy Parker was treated to a lovely

Sunday brunch and then fired from *Vanity Fair*. Dorothy was the magazine's caustic theater critic, known for her habit of skewering shows. At that time Florenz Ziegfeld was among the most powerful men on Broadway and a frequent advertiser in Condé Nast magazines, as well as a personal friend of Nast. The trouble started when Dorothy panned one of Ziegfeld's shows, *Caesar's Wife*, comparing its star, Billie Burke, to the infamously tawdry vaudeville performer Eva Tanguay. Burke also happened to be Ziegfeld's wife.

On a Sunday in late January 1920, editor Frank Crowninshield took Dottie to the Palm Court tearoom at the Plaza, praised her writing, and told her she'd be famous someday. Then he fired her.

Crowninshield had been instrumental in Dorothy's career growth. He had purchased her first poem and, when she was still wet behind the ears and without any magazine experience, had given her a job at *Vogue*. In six years under Crowninshield's watch, she had gone from caption writer to drama critic. Now, on a snowy Sunday afternoon just days into the new decade, Dottie was unemployed. For the rest of her life she would consider herself "freelance" and would never take a staff magazine job again.

The event at the Plaza had another lasting impact on her life. The day after Dorothy's dismissal from *Vanity Fair*, her close friend Robert Benchley, the magazine's managing editor, resigned in protest. The *Times* reported the news, and so did FPA shortly afterward for *The World*: "R. Benchley tells me he hath resigned his position with *Vanity Fair* because they had discharged Dorothy Parker; which I am sorry for."

Dorothy may have seen it as bad timing—the same week, the thirteen-year experiment of Prohibition went into effect. To her credit, though, she harbored no ill will toward the Plaza and returned as a guest on more than one occasion, although her contemporaries noted that she could rarely afford the bill. She would simply show up at the hotel, and somehow the bill would get paid.

Since its 1907 opening, the nineteen-story beaux-arts building has become a fixture in New York lore. The Beatles stayed there in 1964 while in town for the *Ed Sullivan Show*, and author Kay Thompson's famous children's books about the precocious Eloise are set there. More than forty movies have been filmed at the hotel, from *Plaza Suite* and Alfred Hitchcock's *North*

by *Northwest* to *Arthur*. Ernest Hemingway suggested that Scott Fitzgerald (who once jumped into the fountain outside the hotel with Zelda) donate his liver to Princeton and his heart to the Plaza.

The Plaza was the first New York hotel to be placed on the National Register of Historic Places. In 2004 it was purchased by developers and closed for four years. The majority of the hotel was converted into luxury units—some buyers spent $50 million each—and a small fraction of the rooms (not facing Central Park) were eventually reopened. In 2011 the legendary Oak Room and Oak Bar were closed. Those who can't afford a room might want to stroll through the lovely lobby or avail themselves of the public restrooms.

The bonds of friendship between Dorothy Parker and Robert Benchley were exceptionally strong. They met when he was hired as managing editor of *Vanity Fair* in 1919 and she was the magazine's drama critic. They were part of the Algonquin Round Table together and collaborated on various projects with their friends. When Benchley made the switch from editor to performer, they spent time together in Los Angeles. His death in 1945 affected her deeply.

Prohibition in New York: The Failure of the Grand Experiment

During World War I Congress bowed to pressure from temperance groups to turn the nation dry. The Eighteenth Amendment, which prohibited the manufacture, sale, or transportation of alcoholic beverages in the United States, was a disastrous failure. During the thirteen years Prohibition was in place, it was widely ignored. Dorothy Parker and her friends were among those who considered the law a nuisance and continued with their libertine lifestyle uninterrupted. Dottie's friend Jane Grant, a reporter for the *New York Times* and the wife of *New Yorker* editor Harold Ross, had her own personal bootlegger to supply their home with booze. Parker herself was once caught in a speakeasy raid by federal agents. Polly Adler, the city's best-known brothel owner, declared, "They might as well try to dry up the Atlantic with a post office blotter."

Barrels of confiscated liquor. New York City had more than 30,000 illegal speakeasies and nightclubs in operation during Prohibition.

The Volstead Act, more formally known as the National Prohibition Enforcement Act, passed over President Woodrow Wilson's veto on October 28, 1919. The act specified the provisions of the Eighteenth Amendment, delineated fines and prison terms for violation of the law, and empowered the Bureau of Internal Revenue to enforce Prohibition.

National Prohibition went into effect at midnight on January 16, 1920. At that time Colonel Jacob Ruppert, the beer baron and owner of the New York Yankees, had increased the capacity of his brewery to 1.3 million barrels per year, up from 350,000 thirty years before. His business was closed until 1933. City bars, saloons, restaurants, and hotels were forced to stop selling alcohol, but not before hosting raucous parties. Some bartenders dressed as pallbearers; saloons brought in coffins. For thirteen years, drinking bootleg beer and distilled spirits was the norm. Wine and beer were brewed in homes, gin was made in bathtub stills, and illegal imports were brought in from Canada and Florida by rumrunners. In New York City, the number of places where liquor could be purchased more than doubled, from 15,000 legal spots to 32,000 illegal ones.

After a speakeasy was raided and closed by the authorities, it was prevented from reopening by its utter destruction.

In 1932 activists took to the streets seeking to end Prohibition.

In 1924 New York City gave up trying to enforce the Volstead Act and asked the feds to step in and stop the illicit business in bootleg booze. Crime associated with speakeasies and bootlegging was rampant. Beatings, shootings, and stabbings were splashed across the newspapers. Prohibition provided a new way for city criminals to make a living; it also helped the Mafia cement its place in the underworld.

The notorious gambler Arnold Rothstein started a trucking company as a cover for his bootlegging racket. He hired gangsters such as Meyer Lansky and Benjamin Hyman "Bugsy" Siegel to run his operation to supply the city with liquor day and night. Rothstein, who lived at the Ansonia Hotel (2108 Broadway), was the man who fixed the 1919 World Series between the Cincinnati Reds and the Chicago White Sox. In 1924, nineteen-year-old Joseph Bonanno worked for underworld bootleggers in Brooklyn and rose to head his own bloody Mafia family. In Queens, Vito Genovese used bread-company trucks to move alcohol around the city at night. In 1926 Congressman Fiorello La Guardia said it would take 250,000 police officers to enforce the law, and another 200,000 to keep the cops honest.

Calls for repeal of the Eighteenth Amendment began as early as 1923. A three-year investigation ordered by President Herbert Hoover confirmed in 1931 that the amendment was not being enforced in most states. In 1932 Democrats supported its repeal. The overwhelming Democratic victory encouraged Congress to pass the Twenty-First Amendment, repealing the Eighteenth, on February 20, 1933. On March 22, the Volstead Act was amended to permit the sale of 3.2 percent beer and wine. Once the Twenty-First Amendment was ratified the following December, the Volstead Act became void. An estimated 1.4 billion gallons of illegal hard liquor was sold over the thirteen years Prohibition was in effect.

Repeal is celebrated with a cocktail shaker at the Waldorf-Astoria in 1933.

In 1920 Robert Benchley and Dorothy Parker rented an office here at the Metropolitan Opera House building. The space was quite small, and friends would drop by their little room for visits. Dorothy suggested they stencil on their door "The Utica Drop Forge Tool & Dye Works." This building, located on 39th Street and Broadway, was built in 1883 and demolished in 1966.

Dorothy's First Book

By 1926, Dorothy Parker was hard up for money. Despite steady work and the dozens of articles and poems she had produced, she was not making ends meet. A Round Table connection came to her rescue: Horace Liveright, publisher at ❻ **Boni and Liveright, 61 West 48th Street.** He convinced Dottie to collect her work. Legend has it that she wanted money for a vacation to Europe, and a book would cover the costs of the ship passage. According to Marion Meade in *What Fresh Hell Is This?* Dottie pulled together some of her favorite pieces from the past ten years and handed them over to Liveright. The poem that opens the collection, "Threnody," is a classic Parker piece—the narrator finds not just solace but also a social advantage in the heartbreak of a failed relationship. However, her final line twists the poem, and we are again left wondering just how serious she was.

Threnody

Lilacs blossom just as sweet
Now my heart is shattered.
If I bowled it down the street,
Who's to say it mattered?
If there's one that rode away
What would I be missing?
Lips that taste of tears, they say,
Are the best for kissing.

Eyes that watch the morning star
Seem a little brighter;
Arms held out to darkness are
Usually whiter.
Shall I bar the strolling guest,
Bind my brow with willow,
When, they say, the empty breast
Is the softer pillow?

The publishing company Boni and Liveright was located at 61 West 48th Street. The building was destroyed to make way for Rockefeller Center in 1930.

That a heart falls tinkling down,
Never think it ceases.
Every likely lad in town
Gathers up the pieces.
If there's one gone whistling by
Would I let it grieve me?
Let him wonder if I lie;
Let him half believe me.

Enough Rope (1926) was a best seller and a smash critical success. The reception was outstanding, the reviews were good, and the royalties stunned Dottie. She followed it up with *Sunset Gun* (1928), also for Boni and Liveright.

Boni and Liveright was a 1920s publishing sensation. Among its authors was Ernest Hemingway, whose *In Our Time* it brought out in 1925, as well as Hart Crane, e. e. cummings, Theodore Dreiser, and William Faulkner. The house also published T. S. Eliot's *The Waste Land.* In 1917 Boni and Liveright began publishing the Modern Library—classic works of literature in the public domain, in affordable hardcover editions. The series was extremely profitable, yet the company was in financial trouble.

When a Liveright employee, twenty-seven-year-old Bennett Cerf, and his friend Donald Klopfer purchased the Modern Library from Liveright in 1925, the two created Random House Publishing. Soon Random House grew into one of the biggest publishers in the industry. In 1933 Horace Liveright died, and Boni and Liveright was absorbed into W. W. Norton. The old Boni and Liveright building, on the corner of Sixth Avenue and West 48th Street, was knocked down in 1930 to make way for Rockefeller Center. Next door to it was another publisher from the era, Simon & Schuster, which remains today in the same location.

Passwords, Scotch, and the Dog under the Table: Dottie and the Speaks

Dorothy Parker may have lunched at the Algonquin Hotel, but her nightlife was at the speakeasy. She whiled away many a Jazz Age night at the drinking holes of Manhattan.

During the 1920s, at gin joints such as Jack and Charlie's and Tony Soma's,

Dorothy lived the high life as one of the era's leading personalities. Carousing into the morning hours with her husband Eddie, Robert Benchley, Scott and Zelda Fitzgerald, or one of her boyfriends, she would bring her

The door of a speakeasy with a peephole; customers had to be known to the house or be friends with a regular to be admitted. Passwords were common.

Prohibition went into effect in January 1920. This New York speakeasy, in operation in 1931, was typical of the era. Note the peephole in the door.

dog and set him under her chair; if he stirred, she'd slip him half a sleeping pill. Even while sipping drinks and exchanging banter, Dorothy was always observing, noting each detail and imprinting the bits of dialogue that gave her work such life and power.

The roots of Jack and Charlie's and the "21" Club, two favorite haunts of the Round Table, can be found in a West Village speakeasy called the Red Head, opened in 1922 by cousins Jack Kriendler and Charlie Berns. The illegal club inside a tearoom was an immediate hit. The pair moved their speakeasy to a basement at 88 Washington Place in 1925, at the height of the bootlegging era. Called the Fronton, it had a small bar, live jazz, and a kitchen. Among the regulars was the poet Edna St. Vincent Millay, whom Dorothy acknowledged as an influence on her own work. The cousins' wild success forced them to relocate to ❼ 42 West 49th Street, where a row of nondescript brownstones hid speakeasies, brothels, and gambling dens.

The business moved uptown in 1927, and the Algonquin crowd became Jack and Charlie's regulars. The speakeasy had a big iron gate, a peephole, and the best booze available on the black market. The cousins served liquor that came from rumrunners avoiding the Coast Guard blockade—never the home-brewed stuff available in the less refined saloons. Nicknamed the Puncheon, it became one of the most popular speaks in town, but only those known to the house or personally introduced by a Jack and Charlie's regular customer were allowed in. Regulars were apt to bump into Dottie Parker, Robert Benchley, Alexander Woollcott, Heywood Broun, Franklin P. Adams, Edna Ferber, H. L. Mencken, Will Rogers, F. Scott Fitzgerald, John O'Hara, Ernest Hemingway, and any number of actors, ballplayers, and Yale men. It was at Jack and Charlie's that Parker spent the evening in 1928 after her divorce from Eddie was finalized: Dottie was drinking with her current boyfriend, John Garrett II, and crying her eyes out.

Sportswriter, playwright, humorist, and short story writer Ring Lardner was one of Parker's close friends. His home on Long Island was the scene of many raucous parties; Scott and Zelda Fitzgerald were his neighbors.

Edna St. Vincent Millay in 1929 was a literary star and a national celebrity. Although not a member of the Round Table, she did have ties to some of the members. Composer Deems Taylor, with whom Parker had a fling, collaborated with Millay on an opera. Millay was also good friends with Edmund "Bunny" Wilson, another friend of the group.

Polly Adler was one of New York's most notorious brothel owners. Arrested numerous times, the feisty Russian immigrant had a knack for running high-class operations. Dorothy Parker and Robert Benchley would drop in at her places; George S. Kaufman was also a regular. In March 1935 Adler drew attention when she was brought to the state Supreme Court and charged with running a brothel on East 55th Street.

The club was hardly affected by the stock market crash of October 1929, even though its patrons lost millions. The bar owners extended credit to their hard-up clients and issued scrip to use on the premises. On December 31, 1929, a raucous New Year's Eve party literally tore the place up, and with good reason. Rockefeller Center was going to be built on the spot that Jack and Charlie's occupied. Regulars, including Benchley, wielded pickaxes and hammers on the place and began the destruction. Then the crowd, some lugging pieces of

the old place, marched uptown three blocks to where the cousins would reopen as "21," at 21 West 52nd Street. The address of Jack and Charlie's was wiped out by Rockefeller Center, but its general vicinity is now occupied by Christie's auction house.

Dorothy also spent a lot of time imbibing at **Tony Soma's,** across the street from Jack and Charlie's, at ❽ **45 West 49th Street.** At Tony's, Mrs. Parker and Mr. Benchley were able to engage in the type of hijinks they were so famous for. For example, amused by a patron showing off his new "indestructible" watch, the pair took delight in pounding the hell out of it, stomping on it, and handing it back to the owner. "It's stopped," he said. They answered together, "Maybe you wound it too tight!"

Gordon Kahn and Al Hirschfeld's *The Speakeasies of 1932* depicts Tony's as both devilish and delightful:

> *With few exceptions the women who frequent the place are sloppy drinkers. You can tell the hardier female guzzlers because they sit at the bar. . . . Usually a representation of ladies on the loose at tea time, and flirtations with them aren't difficult. . . . Carlos is the bartender. A dull-witted Basque, he is slow on the uptake, uninspired in his work with the shaker and bottle. . . . Straight, hard liquor and cocktails are a dollar. . . . The bar is small, but complete. The brandy, fair. The Bacardis, good.*

Tony's suffered the same fate as Jack and Charlie's: Rockefeller Center's wrecking ball. In 1930 it closed and moved to 59 West 52nd Street, on the same block as "21." The seventy-story Radio Corporation of America building, completed in May 1933, sits on the spot where the original Tony's was located. This is now the headquarters of NBC, where *Saturday Night Live*

West 49th Street was once lined with speakeasies; it is now in the middle of Rockefeller Center.

Rockefeller Center stands on the site of Tony's.

and *The Today Show* are produced. Seventy stories above Tony's old spot is the building's observation deck. This is a fantastic place to get a 360-degree view of the city, including Central Park.

The Ultimate Social Scene

One of the most famous restaurants in the United States was also one of the most popular watering holes for Dorothy Parker and her crowd during the thirties. Today visitors at ❾ "21," 21 West 52nd Street, step back to a time when bartenders wore white coats and the mixing of a cocktail was handled like a religious ceremony. For more than eighty years, books, plays, and movies have been produced about "21." Bar patrons revel in its time machine aura: collectibles, model airplanes, toy trucks, baseball mitts, football helmets, *New Yorker* cartoons, antique bar signs, a ship's bell, and more. Its exterior is lined with statuettes of colorful jockeys, representing the stables of "21" regulars.

One day in the 1930s, after the Round Table had disbanded and Dottie was married to Alan Campbell,

she and Benchley found themselves at "21" discussing their own relationship. According to one account, she asked her best friend, "Why don't we get married right now?" "What would we do with Alan?" Benchley asked. "Send him to military school," she replied.

In November 1945 Benchley died at age fifty-six from a cerebral hemorrhage, and the club, which had been one of his favorites, hosted an informal wake. Marc Connelly and a group of Benchley's friends gathered at

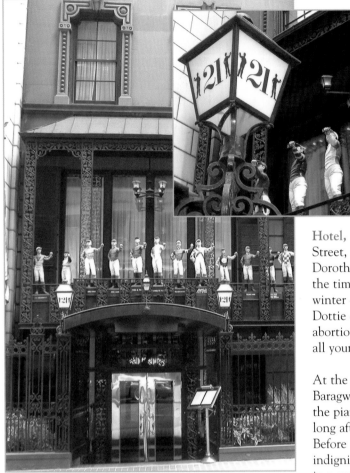

21 West 52nd Street, where the cocktail is king and the jockeys are a landmark.

told Dottie. "Now, Dottie, if you all will raise your glasses . . ." Dottie cut him off. "Raise our glasses?" she said. "Why, Marc, you stupid bastard, it's only three o'clock here, and we're all at work. I meant West Coast time, you silly son of a bitch." A plaque in the bar, to Benchley's memory, simply says, "Robert Benchley—His Corner."

Bathtub Gin Party Place

When Dottie and her pals were tossed out of a speakeasy at closing time, they would head to the ❿ Knickerbocker Hotel, 1466 Broadway, or, just a few blocks down 47th Street, to the home of three Round Table members. Dorothy brought Charlie MacArthur, her boyfriend at the time, to a Broadway cocktail party here in the winter of 1923. He had a wife somewhere else, but Dottie didn't care. He also got her pregnant; after her abortion she quipped, "That's what you get for putting all your eggs in one bastard."

At the Knickerbocker party, Neysa McMein met Jack Baragwanath, a divorced mining engineer. Neysa played the piano while the rest of the crowd sang along. Not long after the party, Neysa and Jack secretly married. Before Dottie and Charlie split, they suffered the indignity of being caught together by federal agents in a speakeasy raid.

The fifteen-story Knickerbocker was opened in October 1906 by John Jacob Astor IV, who also built the St. Regis and the original Waldorf-Astoria on 34th Street. It was one of the finest offerings from the era of lavish dining, with large hotel orchestras and ballroom dancing. When the Knickerbocker opened, New York's theater district had recently moved to Longacre Square, renamed Times Square when the newspaper moved to 42nd Street

"21" and fortified themselves with scotch in a private room upstairs. At 6 p.m. Connelly put in a call to Dottie, living in Los Angeles, who was organizing the simultaneous West Coast tribute dinner at the movie star haven Chasen's, on the corner of Beverly Boulevard and Doheny Drive. "We're here," Connelly

The Knickerbocker Hotel, New York.

The Knickerbocker Hotel, on the corner of 42nd Street and Broadway, was a favorite of the Round Table members. Enrico Caruso serenaded his fans from a window. Dorothy went to parties here with boyfriend Charles MacArthur and artist Neysa McMein. The building is still intact today, although it was converted to an office building decades ago.

in 1904. The hotel was favored by Broadway stars such as George M. Cohan, and Enrico Caruso was a frequent guest. Legend has it that the Italian tenor sang to a crowd gathered underneath his window.

Patrons used to be able to enter the Knickerbocker Hotel directly from the subway below Times Square.

The Knickerbocker still stands, with its beaux-arts red brick, terra-cotta caravansary details, and eye-catching copper mansard roof looking much as they did a century ago. The hotel's glory ended in the 1920s, however, when it was closed and converted to offices. The ground floor, where the palatial lobby once was located, is given over completely to retail shops. Down in the subway by the Times Square shuttle train, a locked door still leads to a private entrance to the former hotel, with "KNICKERBOCKER" stenciled on the door. The door is nailed shut. Because the Knickerbocker straddles Seventh Avenue, it's just a block off Sixth, home to much of the New York publishing industry.

Hell's Kitchen Parties

Harold Ross and his wife, Jane Grant, bought ⑪ 412 West 47th Street in September 1923. The duplex was too large for the couple, so they sought friends to move into the building with them and share costs. Among the communal residents was the iconoclastic drama critic Aleck Woollcott. He and Ross had met in Paris during the war and worked on an Army newspaper together. Through the following years they remained close friends and fellow Round Tablers.

When Ross and Grant moved into the house, Parker, Charlie MacArthur (who would go on to write the hit play *The Front Page*), and Harpo Marx hired a street carousel to entertain the neighborhood kids. Charlie stood outside the house, passing out handbills inviting passersby inside for a party. At the star-studded housewarming party, Robert Benchley was talked into performing his hit monologue "The Treasurer's Report" for the crowd.

The Ross-Grant-Woollcott house was the scene of scores of legendary parties and after-theater gatherings. Parker was a frequent visitor, and

HAROLD ROSS
1892-1951

The magazine editor, who said
"if you can't be funny, be interesting",
lived here when he founded *The New Yorker*
in 1925. At his 1923 "housewarming"
were Dorothy Parker, Harpo Marx,
and George Gershwin.

412 West 47th Street.

so were the other Vicious Circle members, as well as Ethel Barrymore, Scott and Zelda Fitzgerald, and George Gershwin, who performed "Rhapsody in Blue"

Drink Like Dorothy: Recipes for Disaster

Dorothy Parker managed to have a successful writing career despite being a functional alcoholic. That generations of readers have adored her portrayal of drinking and the nightlife culture is a testament to her skill at accurately describing cocktail parties and speakeasies. She even received an Oscar nomination for a screenplay she cowrote about a hard drinker, *Smash-Up: The Story of a Woman.*

The woman knew how to drink. Her poisons were scotch, bourbon, and gin. She glorified martinis but didn't drink them very often. Drinking was immortalized in her classic short story "Just a Little One," published in *The New Yorker's* May 12, 1928, issue:

> What are you going to have? Then I guess I'll have a highball too; please, just a little one. Is it really real Scotch? Well, that will be a new experience for me. You've got to see the Scotch I've got at home in my cupboard; at least it was in my cupboard this morning—it's probably eaten its way out by now. I got it for my birthday. Well, it was something. The birthday before, all I got was a year older.
>
> This is a nice highball, isn't it? Well, well, well, to think of me having real Scotch; I'm out of the bush leagues at last. Are you going to have another one? Well, I shouldn't like to see you drinking all by yourself, Fred. Solitary drinking is what causes half the crime in the country. That's what's responsible for the failure of prohibition. But please, Fred, tell him to make mine just a little one. Make it awfully weak; just cambric Scotch.

here. So much booze was brought into the house by bootleggers that the neighbors thought there was a speakeasy in the building.

Though the city of New York has affixed a small red plaque on the wall marking the house as a historic spot, it is still residential. The neighborhood has gone

Highball

Highballs are a classic simple mixture of whiskey and club soda and can be made with bourbon, rye, or scotch (Dottie liked them best with Haig & Haig scotch). They are traditionally served in a tall (highball) glass over ice, as opposed to lowballs, which are typically served in an old-fashioned glass.

To mix a highball, pour 2 ounces (1/4 cup) whiskey into a chilled glass filled with ice cubes. Top with club soda or ginger ale, stirring gently. Drop in lemon twist, if desired.

Whiskey Sour

One time Dottie was staying with friends for the weekend. When she came into the kitchen, her host asked what she'd like for breakfast. Batting her eyelashes, she asked for a "dear little whiskey sour."

Traditionally served in their namesake sour glass, whiskey sours may also be served in an old-fashioned or highball glass, either straight up or on the rocks.

To mix a whiskey sour, shake 2 ounces (1/4 cup) blended whiskey, 1/2 to 1 ounce lemon juice, and 1 teaspoon powdered sugar with ice. Strain into a chilled glass and garnish with a slice of orange or a lemon slice and a maraschino cherry.

Martini

Dorothy Parker loved a martini—"but two at the most. Three, I'm under the table; four, I'm under the host." (The quip is even printed

"I love a martini – but two at the most. Three I'm under the table, Four, I'm under the host."
Dorothy Parker

on cocktail napkins at the Algonquin.) Her friend Ogden Nash concurred: "There is something about a martini, ere the dining and dancing begin. And to tell you the truth, it is not the vermouth—I think that perhaps it's the gin." All these martini recipes use gin, which was one of Dottie's favorite liquors. Vodka wasn't popular in the United States until after World War II; all true martinis are made with gin.

Martini
2 ounces (1/4 cup) gin
1/2 ounce (1 tablespoon) dry vermouth

Extra-Dry Martini
2 ounces (1/4 cup) gin
1 teaspoon dry vermouth

Classic Dry Martini
2 ounces (1/4 cup) gin
1 1/4 teaspoons dry vermouth

To mix a martini, stir or shake gin and vermouth with ice; strain into a chilled cocktail glass of 3 to 5 ounces. Garnish as desired with olives or lemon twist.

FEBRUARY 18, 1926   Teaching old Dogs new tricks   PRICE 15 CENTS

through decades of change—even its name, Hell's Kitchen, was changed to Clinton (though it never really stuck). Once home almost exclusively to some of the city's poorest residents, Hell's Kitchen has recently witnessed a rebirth; today it is one of the fashionable places to live and work in Manhattan.

Not Much Fun

Dorothy was often the life of the party, even when her own life was no bowl of maraschino cherries. When the bartender at Tony Soma's greeted her arrival in the bar with "What are you having?," she replied

without missing a beat, "Not much fun." This classic Parker rejoinder provokes rueful laughter while laying bare the truth of her personal life: While she had some wild nights on the town and glamorous boyfriends in the twenties, these years were also a shallow and often difficult time. She bounced from apartment to apartment throughout the decade, just as she bounced from lover to lover. The trail of residences begins on the Upper West Side, where Dottie became Mrs. Parker.

The Honeymoon Is Over

In 1918, when Dorothy was twenty-four and on the staff of *Vanity Fair*, she took a furnished apartment on **12 West 71st Street,** just one street away from the house she lived in as a child, at 214 West 72nd Street. Maybe she wanted the security of living in the old neighborhood because she would be living here alone while her husband, Eddie, was in the army.

This is the kind of apartment that a solitary woman, her husband away in the army, occupies in stories such as "The Lovely Leave" (1943) and the poem "The Small Hours" (1926):

> *No more my little song comes back;*
> *And now of nights I lay*
> *My head on down, to watch the black*
> *And wait the unfailing gray.*
>
> *Oh, sad are winter nights, and slow;*
> *And sad's a song that's dumb;*
> *And sad it is to lie and know*
> *Another dawn will come.*

After Eddie returned from the war, the couple lived here together until 1920. This apartment proved too glum for them, though, so the couple eventually moved—not too far, however.

Dorothy and Eddie on the Skids

The postwar Parkers didn't get along, for a variety of reasons. Whereas Dorothy was a discerning drama critic with impossibly high standards, her husband preferred the "leg and fanny shows" that were popular at the time. No match for the wits at the Round Table, he became the butt of many of Dorothy's jokes. Eddie returned to his job at the brokerage. Meanwhile, his wife was becoming a national celebrity.

252 West 76th Street, where Dottie began the 1920s.

In February 1920, just a few weeks after Dottie was dropped by Vanity Fair, a national census taker found the couple living at ⓭ 252 West 76th Street, a few doors west of Broadway. They were in one of the many upscale apartments on the Upper West Side. Both were listed as "boarders" in the building—Dorothy in room 834 and Eddie in room 704. Her occupation was listed as "Writer, magazines," and his was "Broker." The couple moved to West 57th Street not long after this, but a change of apartments could not help this marriage.

Bad Marriage, Bad Apartment

Dorothy and Eddie Parker spent their unhappiest times at ⓮ 57 West 57th Street. The building is on the corner of one of the busiest streets in Midtown.

Their marriage on the rocks, the couple resided here briefly in the early 1920s before they split up for good. Dorothy used her time here to mine for future stories and verse. In those days, the Sixth Avenue subway was elevated, not underground like it is today. This was a noisy, sooty street, and the Parkers would have had to shout to be heard at times—and shout they did. They had a rented flat on the top floor of the shabby three-story red-brick building. The building was really a commercial property for artists who needed studio space but lived elsewhere. It must have been dreary with the train running practically on top of it—certainly no place for a writer. Yet Dorothy managed to write pieces there for *Life*, the *Saturday Evening Post*, and *Ladies' Home Journal*.

Another resident of the building was Neysa McMein, who became a friend of Parker and painted her portrait in 1922. The Round Tablers often came to Neysa's

Dorothy and Eddie's neighborhood in 1920. At the southwest corner of Sixth Avenue and 57th Street, looking north, is the elevated train, which cast the area in shadow. The Parkers had an apartment in a commercial building on the corner, where Neysa McMein also had her art studio.

Parker Packs for Paris

In February 1926, at the height of the Round Table's fame, the USS *President Roosevelt* took Dorothy Parker, Robert Benchley, and Ernest Hemingway to France. Dorothy was having an affair with publisher Seward Collins and wanted a break. She decided that living in Europe appealed to her and so, with the dollar strong, she booked passage on the same luxury liner that Hemingway was sailing on. Benchley, never one to miss a party, talked his wife into letting him sail with them. The ship was full, and he didn't even have a room when they departed, but he managed to bunk somewhere. The group boarded on a freezing night at the docks in Hoboken and sailed to Cherbourg. The trio passed the time playing card games, dining in the officers' mess, and telling stories.

Ernest Hemingway in the 1920s, about the time that *The Sun Also Rises* came out. He met Dorothy in Manhattan and sailed with her and Benchley to Paris in 1926. Hemingway gave her tours of Paris and Spain and took her to a bullfight, whose shocking violence and bloodshed made her sick. Unfortunately, Hemingway later turned on Dorothy, writing a mean-spirited satirical poem in which he called her "the tragic poetess" and made light of her suicide attempts.

studio for drinks. Downstairs was the Swiss Alps, a restaurant that sent dinners up to Dorothy, who couldn't even boil an egg.

The Parkers separated in 1922 and took another six years to finalize their divorce. Mrs. Parker was probably among the last tenants of the building on West 57th, which was knocked down in the late twenties for the monster-size office building that still stands there.

Scott, Zelda, and Scottie Fitzgerald, Christmas 1925. The couple met Dottie in New York, when Scott's star was rising, soon after their marriage. Dottie adored Scott, though she was not fond of Zelda. Through the Fitzgeralds, on the French Riviera she met Gerald and Sara Murphy, with whom she later traveled in Europe.

Dottie in Distress

One of Parker's love affairs in the mid-1920s was with Seward "Sewie" Collins, a friend of Edmund Wilson's from Princeton. Collins had a brief magazine career until he bought a small literary publication, *The Bookman*. He used his position as publisher to woo Dottie, who become enamored with him, to the point of giving him first crack at two of her most famous stories: "A Telephone Call" (January 1928) and "Big Blonde" (February 1929). After carrying on a rocky and turbulent relationship with Collins for months, by early 1927 Dorothy was exhausted. On March 25, her sister, Helen, sent a one-sentence telegram to Collins, which was delivered to him at the Breakers in Palm Beach:

Dorothy very ill heart and nerve prostration due to your telegram please send her nice message

Over the course of that winter, Collins had gone from Paris to Palm Beach and on to Pasadena, California, to get away from the fragile writer. Dorothy, unable to recover from yet another failed romance, checked into ⑮ **Presbyterian Hospital,** at **41 East 70th Street,** between Park and Madison avenues. Four days later, Collins was handed another telegram, this one from Dorothy, as he lounged at the luxury hotel:

41 East 70th Street; Parker the patient rested here.

Seems heart has sprung leak own volition. Would have several little Dutch boys hold their thumbs there. But they say must be long rest here and then can only be half person never one of boys again. Guess that was not so important was it. . . . Doctor working with me mentally and don't mean Christian Science or analysis. Trying to get me out of sense of shame that blocks work like stone wall. Maybe someday can be useful and even self-respecting person. Promise never send you blue word again. But now seems long road ahead. Your friendship loveliest thing. Please let me be confident of it.

In May 1927 she wrote to him:

This is my favorite hospital and everybody is very brisk and sterilized and kind and nice. But they are always sticking thermometers into you or turning lights on you or instructing you in occupational therapy (rug-making—there's a fascinating pursuit!) and you don't get a chance to gather any news for letter-writing.

Of course, if I thought you would listen, I could tell you about the cunning little tot of four who ran up and down the corridor all day long; and I think, from the way he sounded, he had his little horse-shoes on. Some well-wisher had given him a set of keys to play with, and he jingled them as he ran, and just as he came to my door, the manly little fellow would drop them. And when I got so I knew when to expect the crash, he'd fool me and run by two and even three times without letting them go. Well, they took him up and operated on his shoulder, and they don't think he will ever be able to use his right arm again. So that will stop that God damn nonsense.

Dottie-the-Pooh

British author A. A. Milne was a thorn in Dorothy Parker's side. In October 1928, while reviewing his latest book for *The New Yorker* as "Constant Reader," she composed one of her most memorable lines: "And it is that word 'hummy,' my darlings, that marks the first place in *The House at Pooh Corner* at which Tonstant Weader fwowed up." Her dislike of Milne's work ran deep. Her publisher, Boni and Liveright, tried to market Dottie as "Milne-like." She replied with "When We Were Very Sore," with the subtitle "Lines on Discovering You Have Been Advertised as America's A. A. Milne." This came out in FPA's *New York World* column on March 10, 1927:

> Dotty had
> Great Big
> Visions of
> Quietude.
> Dotty saw an
> Ad, and it
> Left her
> Flat.
> Dotty had a
> Great Big
> Snifter of Cyanide.
> And that (said Dotty)
> Is that.

(This did not prevent Robert Benchley from nicknaming her "Dottie-the-Pooh.")

And then there is the nurse who tells me she is afraid she is an incorrigible flirt, but somehow she just can't help it. She also pronounces "picturesque" picture-skew, and "unique" un-i-kew, and it is amazing how often she manages to introduce these wows into her conversation, leading the laughter herself. Also, when she leaves the room, she says, "See you anon." I have not shot her yet. Maybe Monday.

Presbyterian Hospital was founded in 1868 by James Lenox, a prominent New Yorker, who also helped establish the New York Public Library with John Jacob Astor. In 1997 the hospital merged with New York

The meeting of two Dorothys in 1931: Dottie enjoying tea with advice columnist Dorothy Dix (real name: Elizabeth Meriwether Gilmer) and her dog. Dix was both the highest-paid and most widely read female newspaper writer of the era, with an audience of more than 60 million readers.

Hospital, the second-oldest hospital in the country, which had opened in 1771 under an English royal charter granted by King George III. Today the site of the former Presbyterian Hospital is home to the Century Foundation, a public policy think tank.

Working through Writer's Block

While living at the Algonquin Hotel in February 1932, Parker attempted suicide by swallowing barbiturates.

The Lowell, 28 East 63rd Street.

She was distraught over her most recent breakup, with her young playboy companion John McClain. Though she had recently published a third collection of verse, *Death and Taxes*, which was selling well, privately she referred to the preceding twelve months as "this year of hell."

In an attempt to turn her life around, Dorothy left the Algonquin suite and took a furnished apartment at ⓰ the Lowell, at 28 East 63rd Street. This was yet another residential hotel apartment; she favored this sort of apartment because she had few (if any) domestic skills, possessed no furniture, and traveled frequently. The seventeen-story building came with maid service, a fully equipped kitchen—which Dottie ignored—a working wood-burning fireplace, and a terrace.

After moving into the Lowell, Dottie produced some of the best short stories of her career. She would ask friends to come over and sit with her for three or four hours and force her to stay focused and keep writing. While the friends occupied themselves, Dottie sat and labored over her desk, writing in longhand. Among the classics from this period are "Lady with a Lamp," "Dusk before Fireworks," "Horsie," and "The Waltz," all of which were published in 1932–33 in *Harper's Bazaar* or *The New Yorker*. Dottie was forced to keep writing because she was broke. The Lowell, a fairly new art deco building, was quite beyond her means, but the managers let her stay because they liked the publicity that came with having a famous writer in residence.

Today the Lowell is a luxury boutique hotel, catering to those who don't mind spending $600 to $2,000 a night. When Madonna lived there for nine months, she asked the management to convert part of her suite into a private gym. They complied.

New Leaf, New Life, and Good-bye, NYC

The year 1933 was a turning point in Dorothy Parker's life. With the nation deep in the Depression, the Algonquin Round Table long gone, and her close friends scattered to the winds, Dottie was about to abandon her familiar lifestyle.

That year, at age forty-one, Dottie was introduced to Alan Campbell, a thirty-year-old bit-part actor and writer. At the time she had all but ceased writing verse, completing only two or three pieces a year. She'd spent two years living in Switzerland with Gerald and Sara Murphy and was floating through New York parties and social events. When Alan got a part in a play, she left the Lowell and rented an apartment at ⓱ 444 East 52nd Street with him.

Art deco gem of a residence, 444 East 52nd Street

The red-brick apartment, built in 1929, is between Sutton Place and Beekman Place— one of the poshest spots in the city. Parker complained that it was "far enough east to plant tea," but across the street was Aleck Woollcott's apartment (which she had dubbed Wit's End), so she was close to at least one former member of the Round Table. When she and Alan moved in together, they adopted two dogs, Bedlington terriers named Wolf and Cora, neither of which they bothered to train.

While living here, Dottie and Alan socialized with the writer

John O'Hara and Sara and Gerald Murphy, and Hemingway was in their circle of friends when he was in town. Dottie also spent time with Scott Fitzgerald while he was getting ready to publish his masterpiece *Tender Is the Night*, which features characters based on the Murphys. At the time, Zelda was at a treatment facility on the Hudson, and Scott and Dorothy painted the town in her absence.

Newlyweds Alan Campbell and Dorothy Parker in Denver, June 1934. The couple lived in Denver when Alan took a position with Elitch Gardens, the oldest summer stock theater in the country. When the couple arrived in town, they fibbed to reporters that they were married. On June 18, 1934, they sneaked across the state line to marry in New Mexico.

In early 1934 Dorothy made appearances on Woollcott's CBS radio show, *The Town Crier*, while deciding what to do next. When Alan joined a summer theater company in Denver, they packed up the dogs and went west. After being hounded by reporters about their relationship, the couple tied the knot in a civil ceremony in Raton, New Mexico. Once the season ended at the Elitch Gardens in Denver, they bought a Ford flivver and kept on going west to Hollywood, to begin a screenwriting career.

Today the magnificent art deco gem where they ended their New York chapter appears not to have aged. It is ten stories tall and is capped with three stone thunderbirds, quoins, and fine decorative details. This quiet street is a dead end, overlooking the edge of the island, FDR Drive, and the East River, and looks much the same as when Parker and Fitzgerald tumbled out of a taxicab there in the 1930s.

Chapter 4
The Aisle Seat
Dorothy Parker as Theater Critic

Times Square in 1918, looking west from Seventh Avenue and 42nd Street. The New Amsterdam Theatre, home to the Ziegfeld Follies, is on the left. Across the street is the Rialto Theatre, New York's first grand movie palace, which was demolished in 1935.

S ome of the most colorful chapters in Dorothy Parker's life were written during her tenure as a drama critic, first at *Vanity Fair*, where she made her reputation as the only female theater critic on Broadway, and later at *Ainslee's* and *The New Yorker*. She was certainly not the fairest or most kindhearted reviewer, but few critics have surpassed her wit in the years since she first took up the aisle seat.

When *Vanity Fair* drama critic P. G. "Plum" Wodehouse told Frank Crowninshield that he was taking a leave of absence, the editor did not cast a wide net for a replacement. He had known Dorothy since 1914. She had come to his staff after more than two years at *Vogue*, working her way up to more important writing and editing chores. Some touch of editorial genius prompted Crownie to give his office wisecracker the job as drama critic. So what if all she knew about live theater was what she had observed as a paying

Times Square.

customer? For him to put all his faith and trust in her was a big step, considering that at the time *Vanity Fair* was the most successful magazine in the country. She took on the role in April 1918 and lasted until 1920.

After leaving the employ of *Vanity Fair*, Parker was snapped up by the editors at *Ainslee's*, who promptly installed her as drama critic. This monthly magazine, which began in the 1890s, published fiction by some of the greats of the early twentieth century: O. Henry, Jack London, Bret Harte, Stephen Crane. Her column, "In Broadway Playhouses," first appeared in May 1920, and she reviewed shows monthly through the middle of 1923, when the magazine started to run out of steam shortly before it folded.

Parker took a break from dramatic criticism for eight years; it took her dear friend Robert Benchley to lure her back. From February to April 1931 she substituted for him while he worked on motion picture shorts, writing a weekly column for *The New Yorker*.

Parker produced a monthly column for *Vanity Fair* and then *Ainslee's* for five years, from 1918 to 1923, attending as many as six shows a week. She attended the opening nights of classics by Eugene O'Neill, reviewed Al Jolson in blackface, and saw Will Rogers and W. C. Fields debut. She used her powers of observation to isolate the small but telling details of a performance, from the make of a dress to the speed of a speech. However, even at her dismissive best (as in her demolition of the play *The House Beautiful* at the Apollo Theatre), Dorothy's love and understanding of the theater was clear—it was just that her standards were so high. For example, in her January 1919 review of *Tiger! Tiger!* at the Belasco, Dorothy waxed nostalgic for an earlier time (which, for her, meant primarily the days of Maude Adams as Peter Pan) and declared the current state of the theater to be in crisis:

Often, in those long quiet hours when I am caught in a subway block, or sitting in the dentist's antechamber, or waiting for a Broadway car, I ponder sadly on the good old times that have passed beyond recall. Those were the happy days—the days when people rushed gladly to the theater, enjoyed every minute of it, applauded enthusiastically, wished there were more, and came out wreathed in smiles to spread abroad the glad tidings that "The show was great!" Why, some of them even, of their own free will, went back to see the same play over and over again. Yes, those were undoubtedly the days.

Think how hideously different things are now. We go heroically to the theater, hoping always, with piteous faith, that maybe it won't be so bad after all—yet ever dreading, with the bitter fear born of cruel experience, that probably it will be worse.

This was a bold statement for a twenty-five-year-old rookie in her second year as New York's only female theater critic, but this was the way Dorothy did everything: without pulling any punches. It is part of why she held such an important position in the energetic and exciting world of New York theater.

Broadway during the 1910s and 1920s was quite different from what it is today. Close to eighty theaters were in operation, with as many as seven shows debuting on the same night. Without competition from talking pictures or television, live theater was the most popular form of public entertainment available. When Dottie began her career as a critic, it was a heady time on Broadway. Ethel Barrymore was onstage; the first Pulitzer Prize for drama was awarded to Jesse Lynch Williams for the comedy *Why Marry?* Over at the musical theaters, audiences could see twenty-six-year-old Brooklyn native Mae West at the Shubert;

Dorothy Parker's Greatest Hits

About Lillian Lorraine, in a review of *Follies of 1918* at the New Amsterdam Theatre for *Vanity Fair* (August 1918): "Most of the numbers are entrusted to Lillian Lorraine, who is easier than ever to look at and harder than ever to listen to. Something really ought to be done about those high notes which she insists upon taking at the end of every song. After spending almost an entire evening in listening to her sing, I can't understand why she doesn't go into the movies."

About Dorothy MacKaye in a review of *Getting Gertie's Garter* at the Republic Theatre for *Ainslee's* (November 1921): "Miss MacKaye's best moments were those when she was off stage."

About Hazel Dawn in a review of *The Demi-Virgin* at the Times Square Theatre for *Ainslee's* (February 1922): "Miss Dawn has gone a long way since her *Pink Lady* days: a long way down. She has dashed through a succession of bedroom farces, extending over several seasons. One might say of her in *The Demi-Virgin*: that she has gone from bed to worse."

About Lowell Sherman in a review of *Morphia* at the Eltinge Theatre for *Ainslee's* (June 1923): "Mr. Sherman gets the utmost out of the addict's spell of longing for his dose of morphine. So whole-heartedly does he throw himself into the role that sensitive members of the audience presently begin to grimace and jerk in unison with him. After awhile, look out for this one, it's going to be a nifty, you can't tell twitch is twitch."

Dorothy Parker wrote more Broadway reviews for *Ainslee's* than for any other magazine.

Al Jolson, Marilyn Miller, and Fred and Adele Astaire at the Winter Garden; Will Rogers and W. C. Fields at the New Amsterdam in the Ziegfeld Follies.

After World War II many of the old Broadway theaters were razed to make way for new development. During the "Broadway Massacre" in 1982, five old theaters were knocked down together in order to build the Marriott Marquis hotel. Today, however, the business of Broadway is robust again; in the 1984–85 season, 7.34 million tickets were sold, for a box office of $209 million, according to the League of American Theatres and Producers. Nearly thirty years later, the 2011–12 season saw 12.33 million tickets sold, earning $1.1 billion. Since Dottie's Broadway days, though, the number of productions has dropped dramatically; in the early twenties there were seventy-seven theaters in operation; today there are about thirty-five. The 1929–30 season had 233 productions; by the next season, due to Hollywood's siren call and the Great Depression, that number sank to 187 productions; in 1939 there were 98. The 2011–12 season saw just forty new shows open, roughly two hundred fewer than theatergoers could choose from in Parker's day.

A Trip through the Theater District Past and Present

1. **Empire Theatre:** 1430 Broadway
2. **Comedy Theatre:** 110 West 41st St.
3. **New Amsterdam Theatre:** 214 West 42nd St.
4. **Liberty Theatre:** 234 West 42nd St.
5. **Apollo/Lyric/Foxwoods Theatre:** 223 West 42nd St.
6. **George M. Cohan's Theatre:** 1482 Broadway
7. **Belasco Theatre:** 111 West 44th St.
8. **Former 44th St. Theatre:** 216 West 44th St.
9. **Morosco Theatre:** 217 West 45th St.
10. **Plymouth Theatre/Schoenfeld Theatre:** 234–40 West 45th St.
11. **Bijou Theatre:** 209 West 45th St.
12. **Martin Beck Theatre/ Al Hirschfeld Theatre:** 302–14 West 45th St.
13. **Gaiety Theatre:** 1547 Broadway, at 46th St.
14. **Cort Theatre:** 138 West 48th St.
15. **Vanderbilt Theatre:** 148 West 48th St.
16. **Playhouse Theatre:** 137 West 48th St.
17. **49th Street Theatre:** 235 West 49th St.
18. **Longacre Theatre:** 220 West 48th St.
19. **Guild/August Wilson Theatre:** 243–59 West 52nd St.
20. **Punch and Judy Theatre:** 155 West 49th St.
21. **Lexington Theatre:** 569 Lexington Avenue

Jacob Javits Convention Center

W. 38TH
W. 37TH
W. 36TH
W. 35TH
W. 34TH
W. 33RD
W. 30TH
W. 29TH
W. 28TH
W. 27TH
W. 26TH
W. 25TH
W. 24TH

ELEVENTH AVE
TENTH AVE

Chelsea Park

① Empire Theatre: 1430 Broadway
Built 1893; demolished 1953

The Empire played a central role in Dorothy's development as a theater critic. She had watched *Peter Pan* here in 1906 as an enthralled twelve-year-old. In December 1918 she returned to review another James M. Barrie play, *Dear Brutus*. It lasted 184 performances—only a modest success—but Dorothy, writing for *Vanity Fair,* had high praise for the leading lady:

Helen Hayes.

> The ladies' cup goes to Helen Hayes, who does an exquisite bit of acting . . . she never once skips over to the kittenish, never once grows too exuberantly sweet. . . . I could sit down right now and fill reams of paper with a single-spaced list of the names of actresses who could have completely spoiled the part.

In a twist, Parker's erstwhile boyfriend, Charlie MacArthur, left his wife and married an actress he had met at Neysa McMein's studio: Hayes. Mrs. Parker returned to the Empire Theatre again and again. Reviewing in Benchley's stead, she caught *The Barretts of Wimpole Street* in February 1931, then announced in the pages of *The New Yorker,* "If you want to, you can pick me out of any crowd, these days. I am the little one in the corner who did not think that *The Barretts of Wimpole Street* was a great play, nor even a good play. It is true that I paid it the tribute of tears, but that says nothing, for I am one who weeps at Victorian costumes."

② Comedy Theatre: 110 West 41st St.
Built 1909; demolished 1942

Parker visited the Comedy in September 1918 for a production of Oscar Wilde's *An Ideal Husband.* Writing for *Vanity Fair,* Dorothy quickly pinpointed the flaws in one actor's performance: "Norman Trevor, as Sir Robert Chiltern, seems to have adopted a new technique; the idea is to see how quickly he can get through his speeches. He broke all previously existing world's records in the second-act tirade about women's love."

Because it had only 623 seats, the Comedy was considered too small for musicals or major productions, but among its famous tenants were Orson Welles and John Houseman's Mercury Players in the late 1930s. The Comedy fell victim to World War II–era expansion in the Times Square area, and now business offices stand in the space.

The theater district was surrounded by speakeasies during Prohibition. Here, nightclub owner Texas Guinan is carried out by supporters after beating a rap for maintaining a nuisance at the Salon Royale, where she was a hostess. The feds charged that liquor was sold there, but Texas claimed she was the host of a party and sold only ginger ale. Texas was arrested so often that she often wore a necklace made of tiny padlocks.

③ New Amsterdam Theatre: 214 West 42nd St. Built 1903

The New Amsterdam is one of the oldest theaters still in use today. In 1913, Flo Ziegfeld moved his Follies to the theater. The chorus girls were a smash hit, and the annual revue was a sensation. In 1924, humorist Will Rogers was in the cast when he wrote an article for the *Times* about the Follies. "Was with Flo Ziegfeld this morning," Rogers wrote. "The present show in our old Follies theatre,

The theater as it looked before it was made over by Disney in 1994.

the New Amsterdam, was raided by the police yesterday. He says show business is getting pretty tough when you have to guarantee a raid with each ticket."

While writing for *The New Yorker* in March 1931, Dottie walked over to 42nd Street to review *The Admirable Crichton* by James M. Barrie, which lasted fewer than 60 performances. She wrote, "I have, happily for me, never before seen upon one stage so many discourteous, patronizing, and exaggerated performances . . . all my envy goes out to Mr. Walter Winchell, who walked wanly out into the foyer after the third act . . . and summed up the whole thing in the phrase, 'Well, for Crichton out loud!'"

The New Amsterdam, which celebrated its centennial in 2003, has a narrow beaux-arts-inspired facade and a vertical sign that went up in 1937 when it was used as a movie house. The theater closed in 1985 and was reopened by the Walt Disney Company in 1997. The interior has amazing art nouveau decor, and the lobby, stairwells, and auditorium feature ornate terra-cotta panels.

④ Liberty Theatre: 234 West 42nd St. Built 1904; closed 1933

The Liberty Theatre and *Caesar's Wife,* produced by Florenz Ziegfeld Jr., proved to be Dorothy's undoing at *Vanity Fair.* The play, written by Somerset Maugham, lasted less than three months, thanks in part to Dorothy's review of a November 1919 performance: "Miss Burke is at her best in her more serious moments; in her desire to convey the girlishness of her character, she plays her lighter scenes rather as if she were giving an impersonation of Eva Tanguay." It was this comparison to a tawdry vaudeville performer of the time (or perhaps, as some claimed, the description of Burke's ankles as thick) that provoked Ziegfeld to complain to Condé Nast. As a result, Parker was soon dismissed from the magazine.

Billie Burke.

Dorothy gave Flo a poke in the ribs in 1922 in a series called "Life's Valentines," for *Life:*

> Still we're groggy from the blow
> Dealt us—by the famous Flo;
> After 1924,
> He announces, nevermore
> Will his shows our senses greet—
> At a cost of five per seat.
> Hasten, Time, your onward drive—
> Welcome, 1925!

The Liberty Theatre was open from 1904 to 1933 and then converted to a movie theater. In 2000 the building was gutted to house Madame Tussauds Wax Museum. Inside are wax figures of Dorothy Parker and F. Scott Fitzgerald.

⑤ Apollo / Lyric / Foxwoods Theatre:
223 West 42nd St.
Built 1910 and 1903; remodeled/restored 1996

Parker wrote her most succinctly devastating review after seeing a new play written by Channing Pollock, *The House Beautiful,* at the Apollo in March 1931. Her seven-word chiasmus stands as one of her most-quoted reviews: *"The House Beautiful* is the play lousy."

Channing Pollock

The Apollo, built in 1910, and the Lyric Theatre, built in 1903, stood side by side on 42nd Street. For decades both were classic old-time Broadway houses, only to later suffer the indignity of life as X-rated theaters. In 1996 the Apollo and Lyric were gutted and combined into one large theater. Significant architectural elements and the façade were retained and restored. In 2010 naming rights were sold to the Foxwoods Resort Casino.

⑥ George M. Cohan's Theatre:
1482 Broadway, at 43rd St.
Built 1911; demolished 1938

Heywood Broun was one of Mrs. Parker's favorite people. A popular columnist at the *New York World,* he produced an ill-fated musical called *Shoot the Works* at George M. Cohan's Theatre. It opened on July 21, 1931, and ran for eighty-seven performances. The revue tapped the talents of many, including Peter Arno, Dorothy Fields, Ira Gershwin, Irving Berlin, and Mrs. Parker herself: A skit from Dottie's short story "You Were Perfectly Fine" was included. Alexander Woollcott didn't want to review a show with his friends in it; however, he did want a part in it, although he didn't get one. Dorothy's participation was a summertime diversion, but Broun chose the chorus girls himself and sang, danced, and acted in the show.

The theater opened in 1911, boasting more than a thousand seats. Artwork in the lobby celebrated the vaudeville history of Cohan's theater-loving family. In 1932 it was converted to a movie house, but it struggled because of its close proximity to the Roxy, Rialto, Paramount, State, Rivoli, Strand, and others. In 1938 it was demolished to make way for retail stores.

The old Lyric Theatre entrance (today called the Foxwoods) at 214 West 43rd Street has three busts above the doorway, a link to the theater's origins in musicals. The sculptures are of the light opera composer Reginald De Koven, for whom the theater was built, and Victorian-era composers W. S. Gilbert and Arthur Sullivan.

❼ Belasco Theatre: 111 West 44th St.
Built 1907

Dottie had her knitting needles out when she walked into the Belasco Theatre to see *Tiger! Tiger!* in November 1918. This stinker, produced by David Belasco and written by Edward Knoblauch, lasted for more than 180 performances—much to Mrs. Parker's chagrin. In her review for *Vanity Fair,* she roasted the drama: "There is *Tiger! Tiger!* Edward Knoblauch's drama at the Belasco, for instance. Somehow, I cannot feel that the dizzy whirl of modern life had anything to do with my intense suffering during the performance—I hold the play directly responsible."

The Belasco opened in 1907 as the Stuyvesant, but in 1910 playwright, manager, actor, and director David Belasco bought it and renamed it. He spared no expense, and it was a marvel of modern stagecraft when it opened as the Belasco, with innovations in lighting and an elevator stage. Belasco, who dressed in the black garb of a priest, was hardly saintly. For his leading ladies, Belasco installed a private backstage elevator that ascended to his luxury apartment above the theater. One of the oldest theaters still in use on Broadway, it has landmark status and offers tours of its inner workings.

Dottie wrote a "valentine" to Belasco, printed in *Life* in February 1922:

> Often in the local press
> On your kindness you lay stress.
> Love's the basis of your art,
> So you say—that is, in part.
> Frequently you tell us of
> How devotedly you love
> Actors, public, critics, too . . .
> Echo answers, "Yes, you do."

❽ 44th St. Theatre: 216 West 44th St.
Built 1912; demolished 1945

The date: New Year's Eve, 1928. The place: the 44th Street Theatre. The occasion: the hit show *Animal Crackers,* starring the Marx Brothers. Nearly every Algonquin Round Table member attended the performance and then went out to ring in 1929 together. The show was written by George S. Kaufman and Morrie Ryskind. It starred Groucho (Captain Spalding), Chico (Emanuel Ravelli), Harpo (The Professor), and Zeppo (Jamison). Harpo was close to Alexander Woollcott, who brought the brothers to the attention of his friends. The theater, built in 1912, had its last show in 1945: *On the Town,* with music by Leonard Bernstein. This is also where the Stage Door Canteen was located during World War II—a restaurant and bar for servicemen, where celebrities would drop in and entertain the boys. It was demolished soon after, when the *New York Times* extended its building from 43rd Street.

The Marx Brothers in New York. From left: Groucho, Zeppo, Harpo, Chico.

⑨ Morosco Theatre: 217 West 45th St.
Built 1917; demolished 1982

The Morosco Theatre, with more than 900 seats, was named for impresario Oliver Morosco. When Parker went to the Morosco to review *The Silent Witness* in March 1931, she focused her attention on the costumes.

Miss [Kay] Strozzi by the way, is featured on the program—why, I cannot fathom, save that she had the temerity to wear as truly horrible a gown as ever I have seen on the American stage. There was a flowing skirt of pale chiffon—you men don't have to listen—and a bodice of rose-colored taffeta, the sleeves of which ended shortly below her shoulders. Then there was an expanse of naked arms, and then, around the wrists, taffeta frills such as are fastened about the unfortunate necks of beaten white poodle-dogs in animal acts. Had she not luckily been strangled by a member of the cast while disporting this garment, I should have fought my way to the stage and done her in, myself.

The Morosco, known for drama and comedies, met the wrecking ball with the Bijou and other nearby theaters in 1982 to enable construction of the Marriott Marquis hotel.

⑩ Plymouth Theatre / Schoenfeld Theatre: 234–40 West 45th St.
Built 1917

Parker saw many shows at the Plymouth, among them Ibsen's *Hedda Gabler* in April 1918, not long after it opened. In *Vanity Fair* Dorothy proclaimed the play's importance: "After *Hedda Gabler,* the season was over for me. There just wasn't one other thing that I could get all heated up about. My life was a long succession of thin evenings." She also was in the audience for Leo Tolstoy's *Redemption* in October 1918. As she wrote in *Vanity Fair,* this play, too, had a dramatic effect on her: "I went into the Plymouth Theatre a comparatively young woman, and I staggered out of it, three hours later, twenty years older, haggard and broken with suffering."

Designed and built by architect Herbert J. Krapp, the Plymouth opened in 1918. The theater's patterned brickwork and its interior, based on the neoclassical designs of Robert Adams, make it a city landmark. In May 2005 it was renamed for Shubert Organization chairman Gerald Schoenfeld.

The Morosco Theatre (here in 1981, the year before it was demolished) could hold an audience of about 950. Thornton Wilder's *Our Town* debuted here in 1938, as did Arthur Miller's *Death of a Salesman* in 1949.

⑪ Bijou Theatre: 209 West 45th St.
Built 1917; demolished 1982

The long-gone Bijou Theatre has ties to Dorothy Parker as both a critic and a creator. Parker trudged to the Bijou one night in March 1931 to review the play *Lady Beyond the Moon* for *The New Yorker.* She wrote, "It was a dull, silly, dirty play of some sort of house-party on Lake Como." The show lasted barely two weeks.

Three years later she was back to watch an original production of a play based on her material, *After Such Pleasures.* The play, a montage of scenes culled from her short fiction and poetry, was written and directed by Edward F. Gardner and starred Shirley Booth. Although Parker didn't have a hand in the show, she did have a stake in its success and royalties. Unfortunately, it ran for only twenty-three performances.

The Bijou was one of the smaller theaters on Broadway, with only 365 seats. It was designed by Herbert J. Krapp, who also designed the Plymouth and the Broadhurst for the Shubert Brothers. The Bijou opened in 1917 and was a Broadway theater until the 1950s. It changed hands and became CBS Studio 62 in 1951; in 1962 it showed art films as the D. W. Griffith Theatre. It then switched back to being the Bijou Theatre until *Godzilla* came in 1965, when it became the Toho Cinema, screening Japanese films. It was a movie house until 1982, when, along with the Morosco and three other theaters, it was knocked down.

⑫ Martin Beck Theatre / Al Hirschfeld Theatre: 302–14 West 45th Street
Built 1924

Opened in 1924 and named for producer Martin Beck, this is among the most spectacular of Broadway theaters, and its Moorish-Byzantine-inspired interiors and lavish decoration have helped it attain landmark status. It was while exiting through the theater's swinging doors in December 1933 that Mrs. Parker is reported to have uttered one of her most famous remarks, following Katharine Hepburn's performance as Stella Surrege in an English drawing-room production called *The Lake*: "She ran the gamut of emotions from A to B." When Hepburn passed away in 2003, this quip was mentioned in her *New York Times* obituary.

In the mid-1950s, Lillian Hellman somehow managed to talk Dottie into providing the lyrics for a musical comedy Hellman was writing, even though Parker was still smarting from the failure of *The Ladies of the Corridor,* a play she had cowritten a few years before. Hellman's project was based on Voltaire's novel *Candide.* Dorothy was asked to write lyrics with Richard Wilbur and John Latouche. The others working on the show were all talented, and it was assumed that this musical would be a big hit. It turned out to be a near miss.

Candide opened on December 1, 1956, at the Martin Beck and ran for seventy-three performances before the plug was pulled early in 1957. Harold Prince revived it twenty years later, however, and it ran for almost 750 shows; in 1997 it was brought back a third time and ran for another 100. Dorothy knew where to place the blame: "I had only one lyric in it. It didn't work out very well. There were too many geniuses in it, you know."

The Martin Beck, designed in the Byzantine style, opened in 1924. Beck, a vaudeville mogul, came up with the concept, which was designed and executed by San Francisco architect G. Albert Lansburgh. The theater features distinctive wrought iron and stained glass. It was renamed after the popular caricaturist Al Hirschfeld in 2003.

83

⓭ Gaiety Theatre: 1547 Broadway, at 46th St.
Built 1908; closed 1943; demolished 1982

Like many theater critics, Dorothy Parker thought that if she could review plays, she could write them. In 1924 she teamed up with Elmer Rice, a graduate of New York University Law School who had taken up playwriting instead of law. He had just finished *The Adding Machine* when he agreed to collaborate with Dorothy. Their play, a comedy in three acts about life in dull suburbia and crushed dreams, was initially called *Soft Music* and later renamed *Close Harmony*. It opened at the Gaiety on December 1, 1924, and lasted only twenty-four performances.

Dorothy's collaborator on her 1924 play *Close Harmony* was Elmer Rice, who had already had hits with *On Trial* and *The Adding Machine*. *Close Harmony* opened on December 1 at the Gaiety Theatre; by the time Christmas had come and gone, so had the play.

The show's lack of success probably ate at Dorothy, but she tried not to show it. After the final afternoon performance, she sent a telegram to Robert Benchley: CLOSE HARMONY DID A COOL NINETY DOLLARS AT THE MATINEE TODAY STOP ASK THE BOYS IN THE BACK ROOM WHAT THEY WILL HAVE. Shrugging off her disappointment, she told her friends, "It was dull. You have my apologies." Her partnership with Rice was more than just artistic; she also slept with him—a performance that came no closer to her standard of perfection. Her review: "the worst f— of my life."

The Gaiety opened in 1908, becoming a silent-movie house in 1926 and then a burlesque theater. It was renamed the Victoria in 1943 and was converted to a movie theater. It became the Embassy Five Theatre in 1978 and was one of five theaters demolished in 1982 to build the Marriott Marquis hotel.

In 2010 the Dorothy Parker Society produced a staged reading of *Close Harmony* directed by David Caldwell.

⑭ Cort Theatre: 138 West 48th St.
Built 1912

The Cort, built in 1912 for the producer John Cort, is among the oldest and most beautiful of the Broadway theaters. The small, elegant interior is decorated with French neoclassical detail and murals depicting the gardens of Versailles. In December 1919 Dorothy was here for *Vanity Fair* to see John Drinkwater's *Abraham Lincoln,* which had been a big success in London. For this review, Parker showed her rarely seen gentle side:

> The play is so simply written that there is never a suggestion of the theater about it; even such a tried trick as the soft singing of an off-stage army marching off to war somehow loses all theatricalism and becomes grippingly real, so naturally and quietly is it brought in. The management has introduced the same unseen soldiers in another selection, during a scene in Grant's headquarters at Appomattox, and, though it would seem as if, according to the managerial idea, the Union Army was composed of two tenors and a couple of basses, the effect is none the less telling.

Well-known shows presented at the Cort include *The Diary of Anne Frank, Sarafina!* and *The Heiress.* In 1998 it was home to *The Blue Room,* featuring Nicole Kidman in the buff. The Cort is still a working theater today.

⑮ Vanderbilt Theatre: 148 West 48th St.
Built 1918; demolished 1954

Eugene DeRosa designed the Vanderbilt, which was known for musicals in the 1920s. In April 1931 Parker paid a visit to review Roy Davidson's new play *Right of Happiness* for *The New Yorker.* The show lasted a little more than a week, which was just fine with Dorothy:

> It was a crude, bad, strangely furious play about, as much as I could discern of its theme, the bitter resentment of a cripple for the pity and patronage that must be his portion . . . there is little need, and there would be less mercy, to talk about those who acted it.

The Vanderbilt opened in March 1918 with the Harry Carroll–Joseph McCarthy musical *Oh Look!* Probably its greatest night was November 2, 1921, when Eugene O'Neill debuted *Anna Christie* on its stage, with Pauline Lord and Frank Shannon in the leads. The 798-seat theater was a popular venue for small plays and musicals until 1939, when it was converted to a radio studio. It reopened briefly in the fifties before being demolished in 1954. In 2008 the Rockefeller Group paid $62 million for the property, at that point a parking garage, with plans to develop it.

⑯ Playhouse Theatre: 137 West 48th St.
Built 1911; demolished 1969

The Phantom Legion, written and produced by Anthony Paul Kelly, opened on December 10, 1919, at the Playhouse. Parker observed in *Vanity Fair:*

> Some plays, with an exquisite thoughtfulness, even withdrew, after a brief showing, and resigned their theatres to the incoming entertainments. The outgoing dramas included one curious divertissement called The Phantom Legion, *which treated of death and the author's astoundingly unattractive conception of an after-life. This play holds the season's record, thus far, with a run of four evening performances and one matinee. By an odd coincidence, it ran just five performances too many.*

The Shuberts owned the building from 1944 until it was knocked down in 1969. Today the McGraw-Hill Building stands in its place.

17 49th Street Theatre: 235 West 49th St.
Built 1921; demolished 1940

This theater was the venue for *No Sirree!*—the joint production by the Round Table members. On Sunday, April 30, 1922, "An anonymous entertainment by the Vicious Circle of the Hotel Algonquin" was put on for one night at the 49th Street Theatre. The entire group—artists, columnists, and critics—wrote and acted in a one-night show for friends. Actors, who had often been the subject of the Round Table's stinging barbs, reviewed the show as guest critics for the major papers.

Dorothy Parker wrote a song called "The Everlastin' Ingénue Blues," which included Helen Hayes and Margalo Gillmore in the chorus. They sang, "We are little flappers, never growing up / And we've all of us been flapping since Belasco was a pup." However, the most popular act of the night was Robert Benchley's "The Treasurer's Report," which prompted Irving Berlin to hire Benchley for his *Music Box Revue*. While much of the evening's entertainment is lost to history, we do have the text of "The Treasurer's Report," and through it we can catch a glimpse of the tenor of the evening:

> I don't think that many members of the Society realize just how big the work is that we are trying to do up there. . . . We feel

that, by taking the boy at this age, we can get closer to his real nature—for a boy has a very real nature, you may be sure—and bring him into closer touch not only with the school, the parents, and with each other, but also with the town in which they live, the country to whose flag they pay allegiance, and to the—ah—town in which they live.

Robert Benchley.

Benchley's *The Treasurer's Report*, made by Fox-Movietone in 1928, holds the distinction of being the first all-talking movie.

The 49th Street Theatre was built in 1921 for the Shubert Brothers but fell victim to the Depression. It was briefly a movie theater until it was demolished in 1940 to make way for a parking garage. The property was redeveloped; today it is the Pearl Hotel. It opened in October 2010 with ninety-four rooms.

Bonus: Don't miss St. Malachy Catholic Church next door to the hotel. It is home to the Actor's Chapel. Inside are statues of patron saints of the arts.

The boutique hotel is on the spot where the 49th Street Theatre once stood.

⑱ Longacre Theatre: 220 West 48th St.
Built 1913

After visiting the Longacre many times as a critic, Dorothy would make one more journey here in 1953, for her last effort as a playwright. She cowrote *The Ladies of the Corridor* with Arnaud d'Usseau, a playwright with a few modest successes under his belt, whom she had met at a cocktail party. The concept and setting—a group of lonely elderly women living out their remaining days together in a Manhattan residential hotel—were taken straight from her own life. One of the central characters, Lulu Ames, was a dead ringer for Hazel Morse, the boozy protagonist of Parker's most famous short story, "Big Blonde." To ensure that she would finish the play, d'Usseau kept Dottie away from the bottle and enforced a strict work ethic.

The Ladies had tryout runs in Boston and Philadelphia, then moved to New York in the fall. Among the cast were Edna Best, Vera Allen, Frances Starr, and a thirty-three-year-old Walter Matthau. On October 21, 1953, it opened to mixed reviews. Syndicated critic George Jean Nathan proclaimed it the best play of the year. But John Chapman of the *New York Daily News* had a less enthusiastic response: "The hazard inherent in the slice-of-life technique of play writing is that the slices may turn out to be just so much salami—and this is what

Edna Best and Walter Matthau starred in *The Ladies of the Corridor.*

happened to *The Ladies of the Corridor.*" Another perspective was provided in the *Times* review, by Brooks Atkinson: "The authors are entitled to credit for having written parts that can be acted so well."

The show couldn't make it through the holidays. It ran forty-five performances and closed November 28. Nonetheless, afterward Parker proclaimed *The Ladies of the Corridor* the work of which she was

most proud. In 2005 the Peccadillo Theatre Co. dusted the play off for an off-Broadway run that was much more successful than its 1953 debut. Critic Honor Moore, writing in the *Times*, called the play "as unyielding and coruscating a portrait of women before feminism as I have ever seen." The attention prompted Penguin Classics to re-issue the play in 2008, with a new introduction by Marion Meade. "It's the best play she wrote," Meade penned. "She always used to say, 'Well, I'm a feminist, I'm a feminist,' but she didn't act like a feminist, that's for sure. But in this play she proved, in fact, she was a feminist."

The Longacre was built in 1913 by Harry H. Frazee, who owned the Boston Red Sox and sold Babe Ruth to the New York Yankees.

Musicals played on stage at the Longacre until it fell on hard times during the Depression; it ceased operation during World War II. From 1944 to 1953 it was leased for radio and TV shows; *The Ladies of the Corridor* was the first theatrical show in nine years. The Shubert Organization undertook a multimillion-dollar restoration in 2007–08 in which the French neoclassical façade and beaux arts interior were rehabilitated, the sight lines were improved, and modern amenities were added.

⑲ Guild / August Wilson Theatre: 243–59 West 52nd St.
Built 1925

The Theatre Guild, a group founded in 1918 to put on high-quality, noncommercial plays, commissioned this building in the 1920s for the express purpose of being a theater showcase and a theatrical resource center. Fifteenth-century Tuscan villas inspired the facade. In March 1931 Dottie was here to review George Bernard Shaw's *Getting Married* for *The New Yorker*, starring the celebrity screen star Dorothy Gish:

> I regret to say that during the first act of this, I, for what I hope will be my only time in the theater, fell so soundly asleep that the gentleman who brought me piled up a barricade of overcoat, hat, stick, and gloves between us to establish a separation in the eyes of the world, and went into an impersonation of *A Young Man Who Has Come to the Theater Unaccompanied.*

Dorothy Gish, photographed by Charles Albino.

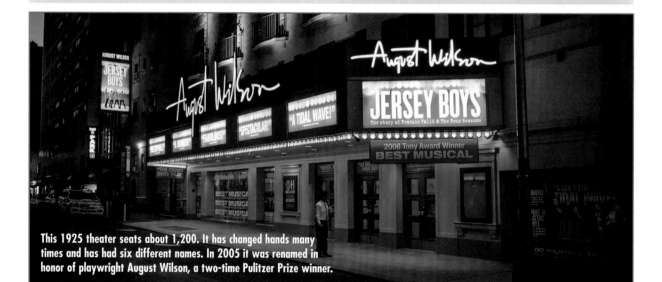

This 1925 theater seats about 1,200. It has changed hands many times and has had six different names. In 2005 it was renamed in honor of playwright August Wilson, a two-time Pulitzer Prize winner.

20 Punch and Judy Theatre:
155 West 49th St.
Built 1914; demolished 1987

After *No Sirree!* George S. Kaufman and Marc Connelly set to work on an even more elaborate production, a nonsequential revue. This time, however, the Algonquin regulars weren't in it; the writers hired professional actors and singers to play their parts. The show was called *The Forty-Niners*, in honor of their previous production. Opening on November 6, 1922, the show boasted original skits by Ring Lardner, Kaufman, and Connelly and a one-act historical drama called "Nero" by the team of Parker and Benchley. Unfortunately, no copies of the script remain. Despite Connelly's best efforts as the show's emcee, it ran for only fifteen performances. This would be the last time the Vicious Circle collaborated on a show.

Dottie also visited this theater in March 1931—after it had become the Charles Hopkins—to review a play by A. A. Milne for *The New Yorker,* an assignment that probably did not thrill her. She had already panned *Winnie-the-Pooh* in *The New Yorker,* and Milne's latest play, *Give Me Yesterday,* fared no better with her:

> *My dearest dread is the word "yesterday" in the name of a play; for I know that sometime during the evening I am going to be transported, albeit kicking and screaming, back to the scenes and the costumes of a tenderer time. And I know, who shows these scars to you, what the writing and the acting of those episodes of tenderer times are going to be like. I was not wrong, heaven help me, in my prevision of the Milne work. Its hero is caused, by novel device, to fall asleep and a-dream . . . and thus he is given yesterday. Me, I should have given him twenty years to life.*

The theater opened as the Punch and Judy in 1914 and remained in operation until 1925. In 1926 it became the Charles Hopkins Theatre, named for the actor, who needed a place to try out experimental theater. It remained in business for only seven more years before becoming a movie house during the Depression. Later it showed X-rated movies until it was torn down in 1987 and replaced by an office tower.

21 Lexington Theatre:
569 Lexington Avenue
Built 1914; demolished 1959

In the summer of 1919 labor unrest swept Broadway, and actors took part in strike benefits held in theaters around the city. This was before performers had union representation, and they were demanding better wages and benefits from the powerful producers who controlled the stage.

While covering the theater scene for *Vanity Fair,* Dorothy was invited to a benefit production put on by the Actors' Equity Association at the old Lexington Avenue Opera House, also known as the Lexington Theatre. It was an all-star evening, which she told readers about in the October 1919 issue:

> *You can stand out in the lobby and be jostled by actors and actresses just as if you were one of them. You can buy a*

> *program—and get your change back—from one of a large flock of imminent ingénues. It is, undoubtedly, an evening to send night letters to the dear ones about. Marie Dresser, Eddie Cantor, W. C. Fields, Ivy Sawyer . . . you can see for yourself it is considerable entertainment . . . the big event of the bill was, of course, the second act of The Lady of the Camellias, done by Ethel and Lionel Barrymore . . . the Barrymores can never fail to be the big event of any bill on which they appear.*

Ethel Barrymore.

The Lexington Theatre was built by Oscar Hammerstein (father of the noted lyricist) in 1914. His Lexington Avenue Opera House was the home for plays, musicals, movies, and vaudeville. The beautiful beaux-arts theater had more than three thousand seats and three balconies. The building was sold to Marcus Loew, who converted it to a movie house for his chain. For more than fifty years it was the Loews Lexington movie theater. In 1955 Marilyn Monroe filmed the legendary "blowing white dress" scene for *The Seven Year Itch* near the theater. The building was demolished in 1959; in 1961 Judy Garland helped unveil the exceptionally bland-looking Summit Hotel where the theater once stood. Today it is the Doubletree.

Chapter 5

Fighting for the Underdog
Dorothy Parker as Political Activist

Labor issues were a major concern of the Campbells. On May 17, 1938, they marched in a picket line outside the *Hollywood Citizen-News*, where the Newspaper Guild had called a strike.

Many know Dorothy Parker as a gifted writer; far fewer know of her staunch support for progressive social causes, from labor unions and civil rights to the Spanish resistance. Contrary and antiestablishment to the core, she was outraged by the powerful who took advantage of the weak. "A good many people, in my time, have called me stubborn" began one of the many political fund-raising letters sent out over her signature during her lifetime. During the Cold War era, they called her worse than that: she was accused of being a communist and was ultimately blacklisted, along with some three hundred of her peers in the entertainment industry.

Dorothy's first public political statement came in 1927, when she was arrested during a march in Boston, fined, and released. She had traveled there to protest the planned execution of accused anarchists Nicola Sacco and Bartolomeo Vanzetti, a case that had become an international cause célèbre. George Bernard Shaw, H. G. Wells, and Edna St. Vincent Millay were among the many cultural figures of the day who had pronounced the trial a miscarriage of justice. Some Round Tablers, including Robert Benchley, lent various forms of support, but others "thought we were fools," Dorothy told an interviewer later. "They just didn't think about anything but the theater." Beginning in the mid-1930s, she involved herself in a sometimes dizzying array of organizations, committees, and speaking engagements.

This work took time and energy that she could have devoted to her writing, but it may have fulfilled other needs. Like the Round Table in the 1920s, political involvement may have given her a sense of belonging, excitement, and importance—as well as genuine satisfaction, which she did not often get from the work that occupied most of her time, writing film scripts for Hollywood.

From the Algonquin to Activism

Growing up in the upper middle class on the West Side of Manhattan, as a child Dorothy was witness to—although not a part of—the city breadlines. In a 1939 recollection written for the leftist *New Masses*, she speaks of how her awareness of inequality began during a childhood snowstorm on the Upper West Side:

In 1939 Dorothy attended a meeting with economist and FDR adviser Leon Henderson in Washington, D.C. In the early days of World War II, she was vocal in her views about social justice, fascism, Nazism, and labor unions.

I was in a brownstone in New York, and there was a blizzard, and my rich aunt—a horrible woman then and now—had come to visit. I remember going to the window and seeing the street with the men shoveling snow; their hands were purple on the shovels, and their feet were wrapped with burlap. And my aunt, looking over my shoulder, said "Now isn't it nice there's a blizzard. All those men have work." And I knew then that it was not nice that men could work for their lives only in desperate weather, that there was no work for them when it was fair.

During her youth and young adulthood, Dorothy's focus had been on socializing and writing. The end of the 1920s brought the demise of the Algonquin Round Table—which nobody seemed to notice at the time—as well as the O. Henry Award for her brilliant short story "Big Blonde" (1929). Soon thereafter, her first collection of short fiction, *Laments for the Living* (1930), and her third and final collection of light verse, *Death and Taxes* (1931), were published.

In 1929–30 Dorothy spent more than a year in Europe, primarily Switzerland, living with her friends Gerald and Sara Murphy. After the couple's young son, Patrick, was diagnosed with tuberculosis, Sara asked Dorothy to join them in the Swiss resort town of Montana-Vermala while Patrick underwent treatment. After returning in 1930 via luxury ocean liner, she lived in furnished apartments and hotel rooms in Manhattan.

In 1933 Dorothy met Alan Campbell, an actor and writer eleven years her junior. Her relationship with Alan changed the course not only of her personal but also of her professional life. The couple, who married in 1934, moved to California and started writing screenplays. They made an effective team, with Alan blocking out scenes and Dottie adding snappy dialogue.

Although many of the films were forgettable, the couple received an Academy Award nomination in 1937 for their work on *A Star Is Born*, and Dorothy was nominated again in 1947 for cowriting *Smash-Up: The Story of a Woman* with Frank Cavett. Legend has it she was an uncredited script doctor on the perennial holiday favorite *It's a Wonderful Life*. Despite these apparent successes, Dorothy disliked screenwriting and often spoke harshly of Hollywood, once describing it as "this lotus-laden shore / This Isle of Do-What's-Done-Before."

In her new life, Dottie gave up many of the

Dorothy and Alan were part of the East Coast migration of writers who came to Los Angeles when talkies were new. During the mid-1930s the couple rented homes in Beverly Hills and worked on feature film scripts.

Alan Campbell was an actor when he married Dorothy Parker in 1934.

habits that had made her famous, trading long nights at speakeasies for long days in studio writers' buildings. She no longer wrote much light verse, nor did she review books or plays. Seeking "roots," she and Alan purchased a dilapidated farmhouse on 111 acres in Bucks County, Pennsylvania. They divided their time between the farmhouse and Los Angeles, with occasional visits to New York.

Over the next fifteen years Dottie was a study in contrasts, earning $2,000 a week as a screenwriter while crusading for the poor and oppressed. After discovering with dismay that the average screenwriter without a famous name made just $40 a week, she poured her energy into a several-year effort to build a union—the Screen Writers Guild—powerful enough to negotiate contracts with the studios. And her 1937 visit to civil war–racked Spain prompted a new round of activism.

Dorothy stayed friendly with only a few of her Round Table chums, including Robert Benchley and Marc Connelly; others, such as Neysa McMein and Edna Ferber, she dropped completely. Some of her old pals thought she had grown tiresome because she was constantly talking politics. For her part, she preferred the company of those who shared her new passions.

Dorothy had the good fortune to visit Europe repeatedly on extended trips. The ships sailed from piers on Manhattan's West Side or sometimes from Hoboken, if the docks were busy. As a celebrity, Mrs. Parker could be assured that news photographers would be waiting for her to arrive or depart. Dorothy and Alan sailed to Europe in 1937. While in Spain, the couple witnessed the civil war up close. The experience would change Dottie's life, deepening her sympathy for progressive causes. On returning from Spain, she wrote the gripping story "Soldiers of the Republic" based on her time there.

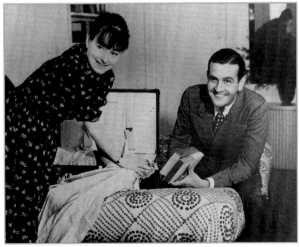

This studio publicity photo was taken in Los Angeles on December 17, 1936, when Dorothy and Alan told the press they were "expecting a stork" in the spring. Unfortunately, not long after this photo was taken, Dottie lost the baby.

During World War II, with Alan serving in Europe as an army officer, Dorothy took an apartment in New York and occupied much of her time with political and patriotic work. She even toured schools with poet Ogden Nash to promote the purchase of war bonds. Her older writing was repackaged and reprinted, paperbacks were issued of her collected poetry, and the first *Portable* edition appeared. Military personnel could read her short stories in a special armed forces edition sent to troops around the world.

After Alan returned from the war, the couple's marriage fell apart, and Dorothy took up with an even younger lover, Ross Evans. Dorothy and Ross collaborated on one play, *The Coast of Illyria*, and a short story for *Cosmopolitan*, then moved to Mexico for a brief period before breaking up.

Susan Hayward starred as the boozed-up Angie in *Smash-Up: The Story of a Woman* and was nominated for an Academy Award for best actress for the 1947 film. Dorothy and cowriter Frank Cavett were nominated for an Oscar for best screenplay.

During World War II, with her husband in the Army Air Forces, Dorothy turned to writing service journalism and pieces for women's magazines. She campaigned for FDR and worked for leftist causes.

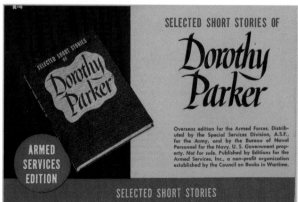

This 1943 edition was among a series of American books that were parachuted to U.S. troops overseas; Parker's friends Benchley and Fitzgerald were also among the series' featured writers.

The 1950s began on a positive note, however. Dorothy and Alan reconciled, and she moved back to Los Angeles with him. Their second marriage began on August 17, 1950; fifty-six-year-old Dottie remarked to the press, "People who haven't talked to each other in years are on speaking terms again today—including the bride and groom." But after just a year they separated again. She returned to New York alone.

Three years after their divorce, Dorothy and Alan tried again to make it work. On August 17, 1950, at their West Los Angeles home, they were married for the second time. Dottie, who was about to turn fifty-seven, accepted Alan's marriage proposal from New York. The couple soon fell into their old habits, though, and the brief second marriage was a rocky one.

Mrs. Parker and the Waiters' Strike

In February 1934 Dorothy was dating Alan Campbell, who, perhaps with her help, had just been cast in her friend Philip Barry's new play *The Joyous Season*. One day she received a telephone call from Aleck Woollcott, one of her best friends from the Round Table coterie, who wanted her support—for a strike. He called Robert Benchley as well. The three founding members of the Vicious Circle, known primarily for their quick wit and one-liners, were starting to "get ink" for their roles as labor activists. This was a role well suited to Dorothy, and she accepted the challenge readily; however, the night didn't go quite as planned.

The waiters at ❶ the Waldorf-Astoria Hotel, 301 Park Avenue, were on strike. Two staff members from *Common Sense* magazine planned to cause a scene by standing up during a dinner in the blue and gold Empire Room when the band took a break. They would read a statement and urge all the patrons in the room to march out in support of the waiters picketing outside.

The Waldorf-Astoria Hotel on Park Avenue.

95

The mission of the three Round Tablers was to pretend to be diners and, at the right moment, march out with those supporting the strike. The magazine activists had tipped off the press and management that a demonstration was to take place, however, so the dining room was loaded with reporters and hotel detectives.

The trio bundled into fur coats and headed over to the hotel. They took a table and waited for the action. At 8 p.m. two activists jumped up and started reading their speech urging a walkout. The hotel detectives jumped on the pair and began to beat them up. As the *Times* reported, a table or two was overturned and fists flew.

Parker, Benchley, and Woollcott stood up and started shouting insults and wisecracks as the men fought. Dorothy asked if it was a private fight, or "could anyone get in on it?" As the demonstrators were hauled out, the newspaper reported that the trio "gibed at the detectives with a running fire of extemporaneous bon mots and 'wisecracks' as Rodman [an organizer] and his friend were mauled. They escaped unscathed."

Spanish Refugee Appeal

Considerably less lighthearted was Dorothy's work with the Spanish Refugee Appeal of the Joint Anti-Fascist Refugee Committee, an organization she supported for years. The group's offices were in a nondescript building in Chelsea at ❷ **23 West 26th Street.**

In 1937, after she had moved to Hollywood, Dorothy traveled with Alan to Europe, where they spent time in Madrid and Valencia. Spain was then in the middle of a civil war, in which leftist forces were battling Francisco Franco, the fascist leader supported by Hitler and Mussolini. Deeply shaken by the

suffering she saw, Dorothy redoubled her efforts to help the anti-Franco cause upon her return to the United States.

She enthusiastically lent her name to the Spanish Refugee Appeal, which sent out countless fund-raising letters bearing her signature. As with the Sacco and Vanzetti case, she was in good company; cultural figures of the day were flocking to the cause. The organization's pamphlet *Spain and Peace* had a cover

This Spanish Refugee Appeal pamphlet (cover by Pablo Picasso) and fund-raising letter ended up as exhibits in Parker's extensive FBI dossier.

by Pablo Picasso and text by Howard Fast, who would later write *Spartacus*.

Dorothy's literary output was also affected by her experience in Spain. Upon her return she wrote the touching and strikingly Hemingwayesque "Soldiers of the Republic," which *The New Yorker* published in February 1938. One of her most mature short stories, it describes an evening in a Valencian café with a group of Spanish soldiers who pay for drinks after the narrator gives them cigarettes. This story has some wonderfully subtle touches of narrative detail:

> It was dark outside, the quick, new dark that leaps down without dusk on the day; but, because there were no lights in the streets, it seemed as set and as old as midnight. So you wondered that all the

> babies were still up. There were babies everywhere in the cafe, babies serious without solemnity and interested in a tolerant way in their surroundings.

The story revolves around the narrator's sense of delicate self-awareness and her characteristic dash of irony: "Darling of me to share my cigarettes with the men on their way back to the trenches. Little Lady Bountiful. The prize sow."

World War II Digs

After their European trip, Dorothy and Alan returned to screenwriting, political work, and refurbishing their farmhouse. During World War II, when Alan joined the army and was sent overseas, Dottie continued spending time in Hollywood but also decided to reestablish a New

A December 1937 fund-raiser featured Dorothy and Fernando de los Rios, the Spanish Republic ambassador, at the Hotel New Yorker (481 Eighth Avenue). After her visit to Spain that year, Dottie served as chair of the women's division of the North American Committee to Aid Spanish Democracy, one of the many causes that she supported.

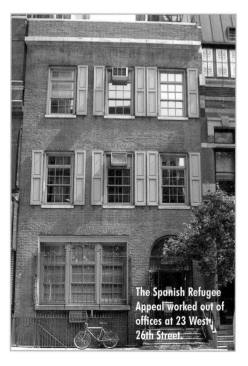

The Spanish Refugee Appeal worked out of offices at 23 West 26th Street.

1. **301 Park Avenue:** Waiters' Strike at the Waldorf-Astoria
2. **23 West 26th Street:** Spanish Refugee Appeal
3. **31 West 49th Street:** New Weston Hotel
4. **125 East 42nd Street:** The Commodore Hotel
5. **123 West 43rd Street:** Town Hall
6. **1515 Broadway:** Hotel Astor
7. **55 West 42nd Street:** Seeing Red
8. **23 East 74th Street:** Hotel Volney
9. **2162 Broadway:** Manhattan Towers Hotel
10. **60 Centre Street:** Supreme Court of the State of New York (not on map)

The New Weston Hotel, seen here, was designed in 1906 by architect Herbert Lucas, who trained at McKim, Mead & White. In 1910 Lucas repeated the design for 1 Lexington Avenue, the most prestigious apartment building on Gramercy Park.

York residence. She chose a two-room apartment at ❸ **the New Weston, 31 West 49th Street,** a twelve-story luxury hotel that had opened in 1906. It was designed with Old World élan: all the interiors were of mahogany and the furniture was custom-made. In the 1930s the Basque government used the New Weston as home after fleeing the civil war in Spain. Later the hotel was popular with British tourists and business travelers who enjoyed the afternoon tea service in the lobby. The hotel was demolished in 1966; the following year a forty-story office building called 437 Madison was erected in its place.

The New Weston was not far from the center of Dottie's old life, the Algonquin Hotel. More important for her new life, it was close to venues such as the Commodore Hotel, which hosted many of the political events and fund-raisers that increasingly filled her time.

Today's Guest Speaker Is Dorothy Parker

Throughout the 1940s Dorothy was a popular guest speaker and host for political events and fundraisers, many of which were held at ❹ **the Commodore Hotel, 125 East 42nd Street** (at Lexington Avenue). Located smack in the middle of Manhattan and adjacent to Grand Central Terminal, the Commodore (renamed the Grand Hyatt in 1980) was for decades the most popular New York location for large-scale events.

A sampling of Dorothy's visits here demonstrates the range of her political involvements. In March 1939 she was one of several foreign correspondents and writers addressing a meeting of the Medical Bureau and the North American Committee to Aid Spanish Democracy, groups that were raising funds for refugees of the civil war. In December 1943 she attended a fundraiser for the Joint Anti-Fascist Refugee Committee honoring Lillian Hellman. In January 1945 she addressed a luncheon for the same committee, applauding attendees for aiding those suffering under Franco. And in March 1945 she chaired a luncheon at the Commodore honoring First Lady Eleanor Roosevelt, sponsored by the Southern Conference for Human Welfare, an interracial coalition of Southern progressives founded in 1938.

Designed by architects Whitney Warren and Charles D. Wetmore, who also planned Grand Central Terminal, and completed it 1919, the Commodore was named

The Commodore Hotel, "New York's Best Located Hotel," was renamed the Grand Hyatt in 1980.

after Cornelius "Commodore" Vanderbilt, who built Grand Central. It offered 1,956 guest rooms on twenty-eight floors, making it one of the largest hotels in the city. The Commodore claimed to have the largest banquet and ballroom in North America—it could seat 3,500 for dinner—and hosted many of the nation's most distinguished functions. Its large ballroom and proximity to the train station made it perfect for public events held by political groups.

The Commodore has a rich history of famous visitors. Scott and Zelda Fitzgerald moved to the hotel during their honeymoon in April 1920 after being thrown out of the nearby Biltmore. When they arrived, they pushed themselves around the revolving doors for half an hour. President Franklin Roosevelt watched his election returns here, and it was here in 1948 that Richard Nixon, heading a subcommittee of the House Un-American Activities Committee, confronted accused spy Alger Hiss with his accuser, Whittaker Chambers. Senator John F. Kennedy began his New York State campaign for the presidency here in September 1960. Before it was renovated, the hotel also had the grim distinction of being one of the most popular locations in the city for people to leap to their death.

An early Donald Trump deal was the splashy transformation of the Commodore Hotel into a spectacular 1,400-room luxury hotel in the late 1970s. The old hotel was completely gutted, and a massive glass curtain was bolted to its exterior, sheathing it in a wall of glass. In 1980 it reopened as the New York Grand Hyatt Hotel.

A Hall for the People

Dorothy was involved in at least one event at ❺ Town Hall, 123 West 43rd Street, a talk by novelist Josephine Herbst about her experiences in Spain. The event was part of a luncheon for the Women's Committee of the Medical Bureau to Aid Spanish Democracy, of which Dorothy was a sponsor. But given Dottie's interest in politics, she may well have visited Town Hall regularly. Long a champion of free speech, this vibrant institution has hosted thousands of lectures, concerts, plays, and other events in its many decades of existence.

Town Hall was the brainchild of suffragists who wanted a meeting space where people could be educated on the important issues of the day. In keeping with their democratic principles, the auditorium was designed so that all seats would be roughly equal: it has no box or obstructed-view seats. Happily, while the finishing touches were being put to the building, the Nineteenth Amendment was passed, giving women the right to vote, so the suffragists had two reasons to celebrate when the hall opened on January 12, 1921.

Since opening, Town Hall has played an important role in the political and cultural life of the city. In its founding year, birth

Town Hall today.

control advocate Margaret Sanger was arrested while she was onstage; in 1929 a commemoration of the second anniversary of the execution of Sacco and Vanzetti was held here, after officials in Boston denied the use of Faneuil Hall for the event. Town Hall hosted poet Edna St. Vincent Millay's first public reading and contralto Marian Anderson's New York debut. Today, the hall is a venue for comedians, jazz concerts, film seminars, and cultural lectures. The interior of this National Historic Landmark is adorned with framed programs from some of these events and many more.

Seeing Red

Many of the organizations Dorothy worked with in the 1940s came to be considered communist fronts by the FBI. As anti-Communism began to sweep the country following World War II, Mrs. Parker and her friends on the left found themselves attacked as "un-American." The FBI investigated them, and government panels demanded that they renounce their beliefs and inform on others. Many were ultimately blacklisted, and some were even imprisoned or fled the country.

In January 1941 Whittaker Chambers, a former member of the Communist Party turned anticommunist, published a scathing article in *Time* magazine called "The Revolt of the Intellectuals," which attacked Dottie, Malcolm Cowley (an editor and friend of Mrs. Parker), John Steinbeck, Lillian Hellman, and other "literary liberals." Chambers charged that during the

Depression such intellectuals had decided that socialism was the way to cure the severe economic problems in the United States; some, he said, had even traveled to the U.S.S.R. to embrace the Soviets and Stalin. Chambers viewed Dorothy as an ally of the communists, though not a communist herself.

When the U.S. government started seeking out "Reds" after the war, the people mentioned in Chambers's article were some of the first to be scrutinized. In 1947 the House Un-American Activities Committee turned its attentions to Hollywood and began subpoenaing actors, writers, and directors it suspected of communist sympathies. Although she was not called before the committee, Dorothy publicly denounced the effort from beginning.

Red Scare at Times Square

Yet another hot spot for political activity was ❻ the Hotel Astor, 1515 Broadway, between 44th and 45th streets. In late 1945, during National Children's Book

The Hotel Astor.

Week, a luncheon was held at the Hotel Astor, attended by seven hundred writers, editors, parents, librarians, and teachers. The theme was "One World" and the aim was to improve U.S.-Soviet ties.

The FBI was investigating the American Council on Soviet Relations and the National Council of American-Soviet Friendship, to which Dottie was lending her name. Thus she ended up in their files once again. FBI special agents attending the luncheon reported:

She said that according to Hearst and Patterson Press the next war would be between the United States and Russia; we hold out our hands to our friends, our allies, our sisters and brothers, the people of the Soviet Union. There is no better way to reach the people of the Soviet Union than by books.

Dorothy then introduced Mrs. Eugene Kisselev, wife of the Soviet consul in New York City, and presented her

Dorothy Parker's FBI file is more than three hundred pages long; many sections are still redacted decades after her death.

with a package of books that had been chosen by American children.

Dottie was back for another dinner, this time to mark the tenth anniversary of the Veterans of the Abraham Lincoln Brigade, on February 12, 1947. The dinner honored the American volunteers who had fought against Franco.

For more than sixty years, the Astor was one of the most famous hotels in the city, located on the west side of Broadway between 44th and 45th streets. The hotel's builders had staked a claim to this part of town before the theaters arrived, when this was still the city's edge and a row of brownstone homes marked the residential neighborhood. The Astor and the subway both opened in 1904. The hotel had a famous roof garden and dining room, the largest in New York. But the last guest checked out in 1967, and the building was then demolished. A fifty-four-story building called One Astor Plaza (1515 Broadway) was constructed in its place; today it is the home of MTV and Nickelodeon.

The FBI opened a file on Dottie that ultimately grew to three hundred pages, although much of the now-released material is hardly damning: Howard Fast's twenty-page *Spain and Peace* pamphlet, a letter from a high school student researching a term paper, and Dorothy's own fund-raising letters for various causes, helpfully forwarded to the FBI by gossip columnist Walter Winchell. But decades after Mrs. Parker's death the government still keeps numerous sections of her file redacted for "national security" reasons.

According to Dottie's FBI file, from 1939 to 1950 she was associated with thirty-three organizations that the agency considered communist fronts. FBI agents grilled her in an April 1951 visit to her Los Angeles home. They reported that she had a "neat appearance" but "appeared to be nervous type person."

Dottie's Membership Dossier

The FBI compiled copious notes about Mrs. Parker's activities before, during, and after World War II. Often it looks as if the agents got their leads from the newspapers, which reported almost everything she said or did. According to her FBI file, she had an extensive list of sponsorships, memberships, and official positions.

- Abraham Lincoln Brigade; sponsor
- American Committee for Protection of Foreign Born; sponsor
- American Committee for Yugoslav Relief; sponsor
- American Council for a Democratic Greece; member of the national board
- American Council on Soviet Relations; supporter
- American Relief Ship for Spain; sponsor
- American Slav Congress; sponsor
- American Youth for Democracy; toastmaster at annual dinner
- Artists Front to Win the War; sponsor
- Citizens Committee for Harry Bridges; sponsor
- Civil Rights Congress; signed petition
- Hollywood Anti-Nazi League; executive board member
- Hollywood League for Democratic Action; board member
- Joint Anti-Fascist Refugee Committee; acting chair
- League of American Writers; contributor
- League for Women Shoppers; national board member
- Medical Bureau to Aid Spanish Democracy; sponsor
- Motion Picture Artists Committee; executive board member
- National Citizens Political Action Committee; vice chair
- National Committee to Win the Peace; member
- National Council of American-Soviet Friendship; supporter
- New York Tom Mooney Committee; sponsor
- Southern Conference for Human Welfare; honorary member
- Spanish Children's Milk Fund; sponsor
- Spanish Refugee Appeal; chair
- United American Spanish Aid Committee; sponsor

In 1950 the anticommunist newsletter *Counterattack* included Dottie's name in its publication *Red Channels*, a report listing 151 directors, performers, and writers with alleged communist sympathies. Ironically, the report was published from ❼ **55 West 42nd Street.** Compiled from a variety of sources, *Red Channels* was one of the documents on which the Hollywood blacklist was based.

Ultimately, 320 people—including Dorothy—were blacklisted, barred from working in Hollywood because of their alleged communist ties. The blacklist made obtaining work difficult, and it also contributed to the failure of Dorothy's second marriage. As the government investigations increased, Alan became terrified that he would be blacklisted by association with Dorothy. They separated again after scarcely more than a year.

Publicly, though, Mrs. Parker seemed unfazed by the government's unwelcome attentions. She certainly did not stop her political activities. In a 1952 speech in New York as chair of the Spanish Refugee Appeal, Dorothy, wearing sunglasses, said she wasn't hiding her identity from the FBI, for whom she "had only monumental scorn." The sunglasses, she told the crowd of 450, were "to cover a nasty infected eye probably from watching these [presidential] conventions over television." After reading a letter from Irish playwright Seán O'Casey supporting Spain, she raised her clenched fist in the Popular Front salute and gave a cry of "Salude!" At a rally in New York the following year, she was again defiant: "It's a short step from being told what to think to being told not to think at all."

In January 1955, a few years after Dorothy was interviewed by the FBI in Los Angeles, agents came knocking again, this time at ❽ **the Hotel Volney, 23 East 74th Street.** In his "Lyons Den" column that March, *New York Post* columnist Leonard Lyons wrote:

Two government men came to the apartment of Dorothy Parker. They wanted to question her about some of her left-wing committee affiliations. Mrs. Parker's two pet dogs romped all over the room, paying no heed to her command to stay put. When the questioners asked about the extent of her influence upon the committees, Mrs. Parker replied: "My influence? Look at these two dogs of mine. I can't even influence them."

Black and White

Long before she decided to leave her estate to Martin Luther King Jr., Dorothy was sensitive to racial injustice. Her landmark *New Yorker* short story "Arrangement in Black and White," written in 1927, took aim at white prejudice and hypocrisy; the story was based on an evening with the internationally renowned singer Paul Robeson, a longtime friend whom she greatly admired. In the mid-1930s she helped raise funds for the defense of the Scottsboro Boys, nine black teenagers sentenced to death for allegedly raping two white women in Alabama. What disturbed her most about America, she told an interviewer, was injustice, intolerance, stupidity, and segregation—particularly segregation.

Two decades later, she rose to Robeson's defense when he became the first American to be banned from television. In March 1950 NBC canceled his scheduled appearance on *Today* with Mrs. Roosevelt. Dorothy immediately sent a telegram to NBC president Sidney Eiges in protest.

Robeson had made frequent trips to the Soviet Union and had asserted that he felt freer there, as a black person, than in the United States. In the Cold War era, such statements ignited a firestorm of controversy. The U.S. government declared him a communist and blacklisted him. Several months later, it revoked his passport; now he could neither make a living in the United States (because of the blacklist) nor travel abroad to give concerts. To satisfy requests for concerts outside the U.S. borders, he resorted to singing over long-distance telephone lines.

In the ensuing years, Robeson's supporters would stage numerous benefits for him, including a dinner on October 14, 1954, at ❾ **the Manhattan Towers Hotel, 2162 Broadway,** at which Dorothy spoke. Other tribute speeches were given by W. E. B. DuBois, editor in chief of *Crisis* magazine; Rockwell Kent, American painter and printmaker; and Ring Lardner Jr. The FBI had an informant there that evening who ignored the content of the speeches but noted in Parker's file that dinner cost $7.50 a plate. The auditorium was converted to a fitness club in 2010.

Dottie Takes the Fifth

A courtroom might seem the least likely place to spot Dorothy Parker, and it was the one destination where her beloved poodle could not accompany her. But on a winter's day in February 1955, at the height of the Cold War, she was summoned to a legislative hearing in room 408 of ❿ **the Supreme Court of the State of New York, 60 Centre Street.** Inside this imposing classical-style landmark, its entrance marked by ten massive granite columns, Dorothy invoked the Fifth Amendment (protection against self-incrimination) when asked if she was a communist.

In the front of the building are the engraved words of George Washington: "The true administration of justice is the firmest pillar of good government." On this particular day, a government panel with an extremely long name—the New York State Joint Legislative Committee on Charitable and Philanthropic Agencies and Organizations— was conducting an investigation of the alleged

2162 Broadway still reflects its past life as a church.

diversion of $3.5 million in charitable contributions to communist organizations. It had called Mrs. Parker to testify because one target of its investigation was the Joint Anti-Fascist Refugee Committee, which the U.S. government had declared a communist front.

Mrs. Parker—who "wore a mink jacket and oversized cocoa-colored Tyrolean hat," the *New York World-Telegram* dutifully reported—insisted she had not known that the committee was controlled by the

The New York State Supreme Court at 60 Centre Street, shown here in 1927, has long been a popular setting for films and TV shows.

Communist Party. She had been the national chair of the organization, she said, which was why all the fund-raising letters sent out from 23 West 26th had carried her signature. But she had not composed the letters herself, nor had she asked how the organization spent the funds raised: "My job was to raise money and that's all."

Shortly after this hearing, the FBI closed its investigation of Mrs. Parker, concluding that she was not dangerous enough to include in its "Security Index." By then, however, the damage to her career, life, and spirit had already been done, and the echoes would reverberate in the future. In 1958, for instance, after *Esquire* began publishing her book reviews, the magazine received angry letters from readers: Why were they employing a communist?

Purpose over Poetry

By the 1950s Dorothy's inclination to write the short social satires and clever poetry of her earlier, more carefree days had essentially vanished, along with

THE LAST DAYS OF JOE McCARTHY

PACIFIC-ORIENT TRAVEL SECTION

WHAT TO DO IF YOU LOSE THAT FIVE-FIGURE JOB

Dorothy Parker's last long-term writing assignment was reviewing books for *Esquire* from 1957 to 1962.

her former way of life. It was in politics that the ever-battling Mrs. Parker found a new use for her wit and insight.

As she entered her sixties, though, Dorothy found herself with more limited avenues for creative expression. Her newer writing, reflecting her more mature concerns, was often thought too serious or polemical. Some editors—such as Harold Ross—wanted her to write as she once had, but she now felt that "there are things that never have been funny, and never will be." The blacklist had closed some doors, and the demise of Hollywood's golden age had closed others, making the task of obtaining and completing work more challenging.

And so the New York life she would return to in her final years was quieter than that of her younger days. In some ways she would garner even more respect and recognition than in her heyday, but at the same time she would continue to face the same demon she always had: loneliness.

Chapter 6

Excuse My Dust
The Final Years

Dottie in April 1953 with Misty, photographed by Roy Schatt at his Murray Hill studio.

The 1950s and 1960s were not kind to Mrs. Parker. She contributed infrequent book reviews to *Esquire*, her final Broadway play flopped, and she faced repeated government questions about her left-wing activities. During the gloomy Eisenhower era, when her lonely life in Manhattan had become unbearable, she gave up her apartment in the Volney Hotel and moved back to Los Angeles to join Alan for a few more years. The reunited pair lived in a bungalow Alan had purchased in West Hollywood. But in June 1963, she discovered Alan's body after his apparent suicide by overdosing on alcohol and barbiturates.

Dorothy decided to move back to Manhattan for good. Now seventy years old, she was happy to return to her favorite city. "You just don't know how I love it— how I get up every morning and want to kiss the pavement. . . . Hollywood smells like a laundry," she told Ward Morehouse of the *New York World-Telegram* and *Sun*. "The beautiful vegetables taste as if they were raised in trunks, and at those wonderful supermarkets you find that the vegetables are all wax. The flowers out there smell like dirty, old dollar bills."

She spent her final years on the Upper East Side, befriended by socialite Gloria Vanderbilt and the actor Zero Mostel. She lived alone with her poodles, Misty and C'est Tout (That's All). Sometimes she needed a nurse to help her care for herself. Dottie had spills on sidewalks, her vision was poor, and her health was declining. Friends were few, but among the most devoted was Beatrice Ames Stewart, the first wife of Vicious Circle member Donald Ogden Stewart. Bea came all the way from East 18th Street to cook for Dottie. But most people forgot she was still around. When Truman Capote threw his famous Black and White Ball at the Plaza in November 1966, he claimed he had left Dottie off the list because he didn't know she was still alive.

In October 1963, a few months after Alan's suicide, Dorothy packed up her belongings in their Norma Place cottage in West Hollywood.

Academic Recognition and Marilyn Monroe

When Dorothy was pushing sixty-five, her peers finally recognized her for her lifetime of work and achievements. In 1958 ❶ **the National Institute of Arts and Letters, 633 West 155th Street** (by Trinity Cemetery), tapped Dorothy for the most prestigious literary award of her career: the Marjorie Peabody Waite Award, newly established to be given to a nonmember of the institute, "conferred annually on an older person" for her "lifelong achievement in literature." The ceremony was held at the institute on May 21, 1958. Dorothy went uptown to graciously accept. Editor and poet Malcolm Cowley, the president of the organization, read the tribute, written by Lillian Hellman:

> *To Dorothy Parker, born in West End, New Jersey, because the clean wit of her verse and the sharp perception in her stories has produced a brilliant record of our time. Because Miss Parker has a true talent, even her early work gives us as much pleasure today as it did thirty years ago.*

Marilyn Monroe and Arthur Miller.

Cowley was surprised that Dorothy was given a standing ovation, not common at the time. Dottie went home on a cloud, with the prize and a thousand dollars in her purse.

The following year she was elected a member of the National Institute of Arts and Letters. She showed up for the affair quite drunk, and her behavior was far from the standards of academic decorum usually observed at these events. She shared the stage with Arthur Miller,

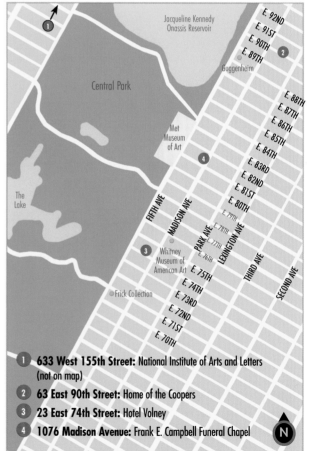

❶ **633 West 155th Street:** National Institute of Arts and Letters (not on map)

❷ **63 East 90th Street:** Home of the Coopers

❸ **23 East 74th Street:** Hotel Volney

❹ **1076 Madison Avenue:** Frank E. Campbell Funeral Chapel

The National Institute of Arts and Letters, 633 155th Street.

A Dog's Breakfast

Dorothy Parker had a lifelong love affair with dogs. She adored her dogs and doted on them like a mother; she wrote stories and poems about them. It didn't matter what the breed was, though the majority of her dogs were the kind that could fit in her lap—just the right size for apartments and hotel rooms. Among the dogs she owned were the following:

- Amy—mutt
- Bunk—Boston terrier
- C'est Tout—poodle
- Cliché—poodle
- Cora—Bedlington terrier
- Daisy—Scottish terrier
- Flic—Boxer
- Fraulein—dachshund
- Jack—dalmatian
- Limey—poodle
- Misty—poodle
- Nogi—Boston terrier
- Poupée—poodle
- Rags—Boston terrier
- Robinson—dachshund
- Scrambles—mutt
- Timothy—Dandie Dinmont terrier
- Troy, aka Troisième—poodle
- Wolf—Bedlington terrier
- Woodrow Wilson—Boston terrier

who was being honored with a drama prize. Dorothy seized the opportunity to meet the famous playwright—or, more precisely, his wife, Marilyn Monroe.

Under a Comfortable Wing

While living in Los Angeles and working as a screenwriting team, Dorothy and Alan had befriended a Southern actor-writer named Wyatt Cooper. The handsome young man was a close friend of the couple in 1961; the trio even cashed their unemployment checks together. In 1963 Cooper married Gloria Vanderbilt and relocated to New York, to ❷ **63 East 90th Street.** This was around the same time that Dorothy moved back to Manhattan after Alan's death.

The Coopers took Dorothy under their wing. They invited her to their home for dinners and cocktail parties and included her in their rarefied circle of rich friends—a social scene Dottie hadn't been part of since before World War II. They hosted parties with her as the guest of honor. She rubbed shoulders with CBS chairman Bill Paley and his glamorous wife, Babe, Bennett Cerf, Louis Auchincloss, Gloria Steinem, lyricist Richard Adler, and many others. She also became friendly with Zero Mostel, who had just won a Tony Award for *Rhinoceros*.

Cooper wrote the definitive story of Mrs. Parker's later years for *Esquire* magazine. His article, "Whatever You Think Dorothy Parker Was Like, She Wasn't," appeared in July 1968. It is the only first-person accounting of the last chapter in her life. One of the most poignant stories Cooper relates is that Dottie didn't think she had the right clothes for 1960s Manhattan high society, so the Coopers outfitted her in the latest fashions. Over the years, Dottie had lampooned dozens of high-society characters similar to Gloria Vanderbilt in her fiction, but ironically, as Dottie approached the twilight of her life, the ultrarich Vanderbilt ended up being one of her most faithful friends.

Photographed here in December 1963, writer Wyatt Cooper and his wife, Gloria Vanderbilt, were among Dorothy's few friends in New York during the 1960s.

Wyatt Cooper and Gloria Vanderbilt entertained Dottie at their Upper East Side home, 63 East 90th Street.

Broadway star Zero Mostel (with Liza Minnelli at the 1965 Tony awards) spoke at Dorothy's memorial service.

One Last Residential Hotel

Dorothy Parker spent most of her life living in rented rooms. Fittingly, she died in one as well. ❸ **the Volney,** an Upper East Side apartment house, was a residential hotel, just like all the others, at **23 East 74th Street.** At the end of her life, this was where Dottie entertained a handful of friends and doted on her dogs. The hotel was filled with old women like her who owned dogs. She had a two-room apartment on the eighth floor in the twelve-story building.

Dottie lived at the Volney twice. In the 1950s she rented a room when she was working on *The Ladies of the Corridor.* Once she finished the play, she moved back to Los Angeles to be with Alan. After Alan's death in 1963, she returned to the hotel for the last four years of her life. When Dorothy turned seventy, an interviewer asked what she was going to do next. She responded with her usual deadpan candor, "If I had any decency, I'd be dead. All my friends are." But death waited until she was seventy-three, when it arrived in the form of cardiac arrest on June 7, 1967.

A housekeeper found her in bed. The hotel immediately called her friend Bea Stewart, who came to collect Dottie's dog, Troy, and got in touch with Lillian Hellman. Hellman then notified the newspapers, and the next morning Dottie's death made the front page of the *Times*, with an article that ran for most of another inside page. The article covered the highlights of her life and included kind appraisals of her oeuvre. *New Yorker* editor William Shawn declared that Parker's life and work

were not only highly characteristic of the twenties, but also had an influence on the character of the twenties—at least that particular nonserious,

insolemn sophisticated literary circle—she was an important part of New York City. . . . Miss Parker, along with Robert Benchley, E. B. White, James Thurber, Frank Sullivan, Ogden Nash, and Peter Arno, was one of the original group of contributors to The New Yorker, *who, under*

23 East 74th Street, Dottie's last call.

Harold Ross's guidance, set the magazine's general tone and direction in its early years.

Hellman had been among Dottie's small circle of friends and one of the few people she trusted. After Alan died, Parker asked Hellman for help in managing her finances. Parker had owned a treasured Picasso, good enough to be shown in the Wildenstein Gallery, that she gave to Hellman to sell to cover medical bills. After Parker's body was removed from the Volney, Hellman dispatched an assistant to clean out the apartment. No one knows what happened to Dottie's personal papers, letters, mementos, clothes, and jewelry. Hellman died in 1984 without telling anyone what had become of her friend's possessions.

In many ways, Parker had come full circle. In an often itinerant life that included homes in California, Pennsylvania, and even abroad, her last apartment was a twenty-minute walk across the park from her girlhood home. The Volney is in the Upper East Side Historic District, comprising the mansions, town houses, apartments, and private carriage houses in the beaux-arts style erected for New York's wealthiest citizens in the early twentieth century. A half block to the east is the Whitney Museum of American Art (945 Madison Avenue), with a large collection of Jazz Age artwork from Parker's heyday.

Excuse My Dust

Dottie didn't want anyone to make a fuss about her or plan a funeral. But Lillian Hellman held one anyway at ❹ **the Frank E. Campbell funeral chapel, 1076 Madison Avenue,** just seven blocks from the Volney. A crowd of about 150 turned out, including Hellman and Zero Mostel. Gloria Vanderbilt had given birth on June 3 to a son, Anderson Hays Cooper, so she could not attend. But Dottie was laid out in a designer dress Vanderbilt had bought for her.

The service began with a violinist performing Bach's "Air on the G String." Zero Mostel told the crowd that Dottie had not wanted a memorial: "If she had it her way, I suspect she would not be here at all."

Lillian Hellman recalled that her friend's famous wit "was that it stayed in no place, and was of no time." She said Dorothy was "until the very end, young and sparkling. . . . She was part of nothing and nobody

1076 Madison Avenue, the most famous funeral home in New York.

except herself. . . . It was this independence of mind and spirit that was her true distinction." Hellman recalled for the mourners what Dottie had observed: "It's not the tragedies that kill us, it's the messes."

Undertaker Frank E. Campbell's five-story building is a New York institution. Campbell opened the business as the first "funeral church" in 1898. Famous send-offs at Campbell's include Texas Guinan, Roscoe "Fatty" Arbuckle, Judy Garland, Joan Crawford, George S. Kaufman, John Lennon, Jean-Michel Basquiat, Biggie Smalls, John F. Kennedy Jr., and Heath Ledger.

Coda: Dottie's Final Journey

Parker had a deep affection for death-inspired imagery. She was asked once to compose her epitaph: "Excuse My Dust," she wrote. Later she penned another: "This Is on Me."

Her will was plain and simple. With no heirs, she left her literary estate to Dr. Martin Luther King Jr. She named the acerbic Lillian Hellman as her executrix. Within a year of Parker's death, Dr. King was assassinated, and the Parker estate went to the National Association for the Advancement of Colored People. To this day the NAACP benefits from the royalties on all Parker publications and productions.

Marion Meade, while researching for her biography *What Fresh Hell Is This?* was the first to write about the mystery surrounding Mrs. Parker's final reward: Parker was cremated on June 9, 1967, at Ferncliff Crematory in Hartsdale, New York. Hellman, who made all the funeral arrangements, never told the crematory what to do with the ashes. So they sat on a shelf in Hartsdale. Six years later, on July 16, 1973, the ashes were mailed to the law offices of O'Dwyer and Bernstien. The lawyers had no idea what to do

Attorney Paul O'Dwyer, who kept Dorothy's ashes in his filing cabinet until 1988, at the Algonquin Hotel the night he turned her remains over to the NAACP.

with the little can either. For the next fifteen years, those few ounces of ash lived in a filing cabinet at 99 Broadway.

In the meantime, Hellman went to court to fight the NAACP over Parker's literary estate. She was sure that Parker had intended to give her a huge sum of money

Dorothy Parker's ashes are lowered into a memorial by NAACP executive director Benjamin Hooks (kneeling) and Kurt Schmoke, the mayor of Baltimore, on October 20, 1988. The memorial is outside NAACP headquarters in Baltimore. A round urn with an inscription on the top holds the ashes.

but that, in the end, Dorothy "must have been drunk" when she wrote the will. Hellman was adamant that she get Parker's copyrights, but she lost in 1972 when a judge ruled that she should be removed from executorship. She came out of the mess painted as a racist.

In 1988 Mrs. Parker's ashes still were unclaimed—twenty-one years after her death. The NAACP received the remains from Paul O'Dwyer at the Algonquin and built a memorial garden at its national headquarters, at 4805 Mount Hope Drive in Baltimore, interring the ashes there. The ceremony was attended by O'Dwyer, city officials, and members of the NAACP staff. No *New Yorker* reporters were in attendance, and the news didn't make "The Talk of the Town."

Dorothy Parker, Inc.

Since her death in the summer of 1967, Mrs. Parker has become a figure of romance, beloved by the cocktail crowd and hailed for her witty repartee. She was not gone long before the tributes started flowing. The first biography came out just three years after her death: John Keats's *You Might as Well Live* (Simon & Schuster, 1970). It is merely the first gloss over her life, stringing together numerous anecdotes and well-known stories but only scratching the surface of who she was. The next attempt, British writer Leslie Frewin's *The Late Mrs. Dorothy Parker* (Macmillan, 1987), was riddled with inaccuracies and errors. His portrait of Mrs. Parker is that of a sad-eyed drunk wallowing in self-pity. The book that rehabilitated her image and established the first accurate timeline of her life was *What Fresh Hell Is This?* (Villard, 1987), by Marion Meade. Meade, who paints Parker sympathetically and warmly, was the first to interview Parker's relatives and record Rothschild family stories.

One of the biggest obstacles for Parker enthusiasts to surmount came from her own publisher. Viking Press revised *The Portable Dorothy Parker* in 1973 and asked Brendan Gill to write a new introduction to replace Somerset Maugham's glowing, warmhearted one from 1944. The problem was that Gill, a longtime *New*

Yorker staff writer, seemed not to like Dorothy Parker very much, not to appreciate her talents, and to think that her work merited little respect.

This introduction to Parker's work, read by a generation of students and newcomers, amounted to a literary mugging, yet it remained in print for thirty-three years, until Penguin Classics dumped Gill's introduction and hired Marion Meade to take over. She revised the *Portable* and wrote a new introduction. In an interview, she said, "I'd felt for years that the book should be revised; at least that the

The Dorothy Parker Society hosts a monthly party with Wit's End at Flute, a former speakeasy on West Fifty-Fourth Street.

Brendan Gill introduction should be taken off. I thought it was a scandal and a disgrace. . . . I had interviewed him for my book, and I personally knew what he thought of Parker: Negative. Totally negative. I thought that is just disgraceful to have this introduction on there."

Dorothy Parker has become an icon. Not a month goes by that a one-woman show of her work isn't performed on a stage, be it in Seattle or Sydney. Parker's lifestyle was featured in Aviva Slesin's 1987 film *The Ten Year Lunch: The Wit and Legend of the Algonquin Round Table*,

Devoted to Dottie

There are two kinds of literary societies: those that study an author academically through scholarly conferences, presenting papers and debating wordy matters and those that celebrate the author in a manner and style befitting the subject while keeping his or her spirit alive. Guess which way the Dorothy Parker Society rolls?

Founded in 1998 in Manhattan by a group of Parker fans, the society adopted a five-part mission: to promote the work of Dorothy Parker; to introduce new readers to the

Dorothy Parker Society members enjoy books, cocktails, and a vintage lifestyle.

work of Dorothy Parker; to expand the fan base of Dorothy Parker; to have as much fun as possible; and to take part in service projects in the spirit of Dorothy Parker. Over the years the group has grown exponentially. The Dorothy Parker Society does not have meetings: it has parties. It meets once a month at a former speakeasy, where "members" dressed in vintage attire enjoy a Roaring Twenties theme party with live jazz and cocktails. The society also sponsors book parties, walking tours, poetry readings, and even dog walks, as well as Parkerfest, a weekend-long celebration every August. The society calls the Algonquin Hotel home, and enjoys visiting other venues

that represent the spirit of the era. It has hosted joint events with both the Robert Benchley Society and the F. Scott Fitzgerald Society— at which the bar tabs were monumental.

In 2005 the Dorothy Parker Society spearheaded the effort to declare Parker's birthplace in New Jersey a historical site. In 2011 it pushed for Parker to be accepted into the New York State Writers Hall of Fame. There are no dues or membership fees; after interested fans sign up at dorothyparker.com, they will receive monthly newsletters with information about upcoming events.

which won an Academy Award for best documentary. But probably the biggest pop-culture boost to the Parker myth came from the 1994 independent feature film *Mrs. Parker and the Vicious Circle*, directed by Alan Rudolph and starring Jennifer Jason Leigh as Mrs. Parker and Campbell Scott as Robert Benchley. Leigh won best actress from the National Society of Film Critics and was nominated for a Golden Globe. The screenplay, which appears to have been lifted almost entirely from *What Fresh Hell Is This?* portrays Dorothy as a lovable sad sack. The film enjoyed moderate success, and its repeated showings on cable television have exposed Parker to a new audience.

Since Parker's death, New York has undergone another of its continual rebirths. Her old neighborhood, the Upper West Side, was on the skids in the 1970s but came back and is now thoroughly gentrified. The stages she frequented on Broadway are still there, although numerous theaters were razed by developers in the 1980s. Most of her former apartment buildings are still standing, as are her school and the parks, hotels, and businesses that she frequented.

When Parker died in 1967, the city was broke, stagnant, and unsafe. Crime was a huge problem, the economy was in tatters, and the arts and culture were under assault. Decades later the city has come around 180 degrees. It has one of the lowest crime rates in the nation, and the economy is booming. New apartments can't go up fast enough, and the sections of town that were Dottie's favorites are the most desirable in New York City. Even her favorite cocktails are back in fashion, with the martini leading the way. Dorothy Parker is one of the most popular authors on social media sites and the Internet. The Algonquin Hotel has transformed itself into a veritable hall of fame for Mrs. Parker and her friends, naming drinks and entrées after them and hosting book parties, magazine launches, and publishing seminars. The owners hung a beautiful oil painting of the Round Table by Natalie Ascencios in the Round Table Room.

HERE LIE THE ASHES OF DOROTHY PARKER
(1893 - 1967)
HUMORIST, WRITER, CRITIC,
DEFENDER OF HUMAN AND CIVIL RIGHTS.
FOR HER EPITAPH SHE SUGGESTED
"EXCUSE MY DUST".
THIS MEMORIAL GARDEN IS DEDICATED TO HER NOBLE SPIRIT WHICH CELEBRATED THE ONENESS OF HUMANKIND, AND TO THE BONDS OF EVERLASTING FRIENDSHIP BETWEEN BLACK AND JEWISH PEOPLE.
DEDICATED BY
THE NATIONAL ASSOCIATION FOR THE ADVANCEMENT OF COLORED PEOPLE
OCTOBER 20, 1988

Dr. Benjamin L. Hooks
Executive Director

Dr. William F. Gibson
Chairman, NAACP Board

Enolia P. McMillan
President

Mrs. Parker's books remain in print, a sign of the worth of any writer. All her poetry and short fiction is available in bookstores today. News writers seeking an easy pun or turn of phrase invoke her name practically every day. Of all the Round Table members, she has become the most successful. The city that she wrote about—gin-soaked and moody, bustling and raucous—lives on today in the hearts and imaginations of readers as well as those who meander the streets of Dorothy Parker's hometown.

Timeline

During her seventy-three years, Dorothy Parker lived and worked in a series of rented apartments, homes, and hotel rooms. Her lifestyle took her to Broadway theaters, smoky speakeasies, luxury ocean liners, and hotel dining halls.

Dorothy's life in New York City is focused on three sections of Manhattan: the Upper West Side, where she lived for the first twenty-four years of her life; Midtown, where her beloved speakeasies and the Algonquin were situated; and the theater district, home to the Broadway shows she so splendidly skewered.

Although thought of as the quintessential New Yorker, Dorothy lived in Los Angeles on and off for nearly thirty years while writing screenplays. She also spent the better part of decade living part-time on a farm in Pipersville, Pennsylvania, with her second husband, Alan Campbell.

1920s

1940s

1960s

1893 — Dorothy is born to Eliza "Annie" Marston and Jacob Henry Rothschild at their summer beach house in West End, New Jersey, on August 22.

1898 — Dorothy's mother dies on July 20 in West End.

1900 — Henry Rothschild marries Eleanor Frances Lewis in January.

1900 — Dorothy begins attending Catholic elementary school at Blessed Sacrament Academy on West 79th Street.

1903 — Stepmother Eleanor dies in April.

1907 — Dottie is sent to Miss Dana's, a girls' finishing school, in Morristown, New Jersey. She leaves after less than a year, ending her formal education at age fourteen.

1912 — Martin and Lizzie Rothschild, Dottie's paternal uncle and aunt, are passengers on the Titanic. Martin is lost at sea, devastating the family.

1913 — Henry Rothschild dies on December 27. Dorothy refers to herself as "an orphan" for the rest of her life.

1914 — Dorothy works as a teacher at a dance studio. She leaves to take an assistant's job at *Vogue* for ten dollars a week.

1915 — *Vanity Fair* publishes Dorothy's first piece of light verse, "Any Porch," in the September issue. She earns twelve dollars and starts her literary career.

1917 — She marries Edwin Pond Parker II, a stockbroker from Connecticut. She is twenty-three; he's twenty-six.

1917 — Eddie leaves for army ambulance training in New Jersey and is later sent to France with the Allied Expeditionary Forces.

1918 — Dorothy becomes New York's first female drama critic, writing for *Vanity Fair*.

Ocean Avenue, West End, where Dorothy Rothschild was born in 1893.

A postcard from the Algonquin Hotel.

1919 — *Vanity Fair* hires Robert Benchley as managing editor and Robert E. Sherwood as drama editor.

1919 — The Algonquin Round Table is formed in June, at a luncheon to welcome back *New York Times* drama critic Alexander Woollcott from army service.

1920 — Frank Crowninshield fires Dorothy from *Vanity Fair* in January. That same month Prohibition begins in the United States.

1920 — Dorothy takes her first job writing for the screen: *Remodeling Her Husband*, for D. W. Griffith.

1920 — Mrs. Parker and Mr. Benchley rent an office together in the Metropolitan Opera House building and embark on freelance writing careers.

Dorothy Parker in the mid-1920s.

The first edition of *Enough Rope*, published by Boni & Liveright.

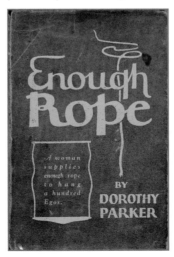

1921 — Dorothy sells her first short fiction piece, "Sorry, the Line Is Busy," to *Life* in April.

1922 — Dorothy and Eddie separate. Dorothy dates Chicago newspaperman Charles MacArthur.

1922 — Dorothy has an abortion.

1923 — Dorothy makes her first suicide attempt.

1924 — With playwright Elmer Rice, Dorothy writes her first play, *Close Harmony*; it flops.

1924 — Eddie moves to Connecticut; Dorothy does not join him.

1925 — *The New Yorker* debuts in February; Dorothy is listed on its fictitious editorial board. She writes reviews, verse, and short fiction for publisher Harold Ross.

1926 — Dorothy attempts suicide by overdosing on the sedative veronal.

1926 — Dorothy takes her first trip to Europe, traveling with Ernest Hemingway and Robert Benchley.

1926 — The first collection of Dorothy's verse is released. *Enough Rope* is a hit.

1927 — Dorothy begins writing for *The New Yorker* as "the Constant Reader."

1927 — Dorothy travels to Boston to protest the pending execution of anarchists Nicola Sacco and Bartolomeo Vanzetti.

1928 — *Sunset Gun*, the second edition of her collected verse, is published.

1928 — Dorothy's divorce from Eddie is finalized; she keeps his name.

1929 — *The Bookman* publishes "Big Blonde," Dorothy's longest short story, based on her suicide attempt in 1926. The story wins the O. Henry Award.

1929 — Dorothy goes on her second European trip, spending most of her time with Sara and Gerald Murphy's family in Switzerland. She returns to New York in late 1930, about a year after the stock market crash.

1930 — Dorothy's short fiction is collected and published as *Laments for the Living*.

1931 — Her third and final collection of light verse is published. *Death and Taxes* sells fewer copies than the previous two books.

1932 — Dorothy makes one more attempt at suicide.

1933 — Dorothy meets Alan Campbell, an actor and writer from Virginia.

1933 — Dorothy quits her post as the Constant Reader at *The New Yorker*.

1933 — Her collected short stories are published as *After Such Pleasures*.

1934 — Dorothy and Alan marry in Raton, New Mexico. They spend time in Denver, Colorado, while Alan acts in summer theater, and move to Hollywood in September to write for Paramount.

1936 — Viking prints *Collected Poems: Not So Deep as a Well*, a collection of Dorothy's light verse. Dorothy dedicates it to Franklin P. Adams.

1936 — Dorothy and Alan buy a 111-acre farm in Bucks County, Pennsylvania. They renovate a colonial

Dorothy and Alan in 1935 in Los Angeles, working on *The Moon's Our House* for producer Walter Wanger. The couple was a popular screenwriting team, pulling down $2,000 a week during the Depression.

Chesterfields was Dorothy's preferred brand of cigarettes. Her preferred scotch was Haig and Haig, and her favorite cocktail was a whiskey sour (straight up).

farmhouse, their part-time home for the next nine years. Asked to describe her farm in two words, Dorothy replies, "Want it?"

1937 — Dorothy and Alan are nominated for an Academy Award for writing the film *A Star Is Born*.

Dorothy and Alan earned their only Academy Award nomination as a team for the original screenplay *A Star Is Born*, which has since been remade twice. They were nominated for best screenplay in 1937, along with Robert Carson, but the Oscar went to *The Life of Emile Zola*.

1937 — The couple sail to Spain and witness the civil war firsthand while in Madrid and Valencia. On returning to New York in October, Parker begins fund-raising for Spanish hospitals. The following year Dorothy writes "Soldiers of the Republic" about her experience in Spain.

1939 — Most of her short fiction is compiled in a new edition as *Here Lies*.

1942 — Alan enlists in the Army Air Forces. He later takes an officer's commission and is sent to Europe.

1942 — Parker is a script doctor on *Saboteur*, a thriller directed by Alfred Hitchcock. According to an urban legend, Hitchcock is seated next to Parker in one scene, but in truth, she does not appear in the film.

1944 — Dottie publishes her last piece of poetry, the strange "War Song," which appears in *The New Yorker*.

The 1947 Universal motion picture *Smash-Up: The Story of a Woman* starred Susan Hayward as the boozy Angelica. It earned Dorothy her second Academy Award nomination, for best motion picture story. She cowrote it with Frank Cavett. They lost to *Miracle on 34th Street*.

1944 — Viking publishes *The Portable Dorothy Parker*, a collection of her verse and short fiction. It has never gone out of print.

1946 — Alan returns from duty overseas; the couple splits.

1947 — Dorothy is nominated for an Academy Award for cowriting *Smash-Up: The Story of a Woman*, a vehicle for Susan Hayward.

1949–50 — Dorothy (age fifty-five) takes up with Ross Evans (thirty-one). They cowrite *The Coast of Illyria*, which is produced in Dallas but doesn't make it to Broadway. They also write "The Game" for *Cosmopolitan*. Evans and Parker split up in Mexico.

1950 — Dorothy and Alan reunite and remarry in Los Angeles. At the reception she tells a reporter, "People who haven't talked to each other in years are on speaking terms again today—including the bride and groom."

1951 — United Artists produces *Queen for a Day*, a movie based on the 1932 Parker short story "Horsie."
1951 — Dorothy and Alan separate again; she moves back to New York.

1952–53 — Dorothy collaborates with Arnaud d'Usseau on *The Ladies of the Corridor*, produced at the Longacre Theatre for just forty-five performances.

1955 — Called before a New York state legislative committee and asked about her politics, Parker invokes the Fifth Amendment when asked directly if she is a communist.

1958 — Esquire publishes Dorothy's last short story, "The Bolt behind the Blue," in December; she begins reviewing books for the magazine.

1958 — The National Institute of Arts and Letters gives Dorothy the Marjorie Peabody Waite Award for her contribution to American literature.

1959 — Dorothy is elected a member of the National Institute of Arts and Letters.

1961 — Dorothy returns to Alan and Los Angeles.

1961 — She does her last movie work, on the unproduced feature *The Good Soup* for Twentieth Century Fox.

1963 — Alan dies of an overdose in the couple's home on Norma Place in West Hollywood; the coroner's report lists the death as a probable suicide.

1964 — Dorothy returns to New York for good.

The cast of *The Ladies of the Corridor* included Edna Best and Margaret Parker.

1967 — Parker dies on June 7 at her apartment in the Volney Hotel. She leaves her estate to Dr. Martin Luther King Jr. After his assassination in 1968, the estate passes to the NAACP, which controls her copyrights to this day.

1988 — Parker's ashes, held at the offices of her attorney, Paul O'Dwyer, are turned over to the NAACP. On October 20 they are placed in a memorial garden outside the organization's headquarters in Baltimore, Maryland.

1992 — The U.S. Postal Service issues a commemorative stamp in West End, New Jersey, Parker's birthplace.

1994 — *Mrs. Parker and the Vicious Circle*, directed by Alan Rudolph, a full-length feature film starring Jennifer Jason Leigh as Dorothy Parker, Campbell Scott as Robert Benchley, and Matthew Broderick as Charles MacArthur, is released.

1998 — The Dorothy Parker Society of New York is formed in New York City and dorothyparker.com is launched.

2005 — On August 21, Dorothy Parker's birthplace in West End, New Jersey, is declared a national literary landmark.

2011 — The Empire State Center for the Book inducts Dorothy Parker into the New York State Writers Hall of Fame.

Dorothy Parker fans celebrate the 1920s every summer on Governors Island in New York Harbor. The Minsky Sisters are popular guests.

Notes

Chapter 1

3: "Mrs. Parker had been cremated . . .": Marion Meade, *Dorothy Parker: What Fresh Hell Is This?* (New York: Villard, 1988), p. 412.

5: "Dorothy Parker is slightly . . .": Dorothy Parker, *After Such Pleasures* (New York: Pocket Books, 1941).

7: "When she bent over . . .": Dorothy Parker, "Mr. Durant," *Complete Stories* (New York: Penguin Books, 2005), p. 23.

8: "A woman at a party . . .": Robert E. Drennan, *The Algonquin Wits* (Secaucus, NJ: Citadel Press, 1968), p. 123.

8: "Her keen eye . . .": Meade, *What Fresh Hell Is This?* p. 32.

9: "First, in virtually all instances . . .": Author's interview with Stuart Y. Silverstein.

9: "I'm reading that new thing of Locke's . . .": Stuart Y. Silverstein, ed., *Not Much Fun: The Lost Poems of Dorothy Parker* (New York: Scribner, 1996), p. 70.

11: "There's little in taking or giving . . .": Dorothy Parker, *Complete Poems* (New York: Penguin Books, 1999), p. 156.

11: "In May my heart was breaking . . .": Parker, *Complete Poems*, p. 205.

12: "I hate Women . . .": Silverstein, *The Lost Poems of Dorothy Parker*, p. 187.

12: "The things she knew, let her forget again . . .": Parker, *Complete Poems*, p. 187.

13: "You Goddamn Christ killer . . .": Howard Teichman, *George S. Kaufman* (New York: Atheneum, 1972), p. 284.

Chapter 2

18: "In an interview . . .": "Dorothy Parker," in *Writers at Work: The Paris Review Interviews*, ed. Malcolm Cowley (New York: Viking Press, 1957, 1958), p. 76.

19: "Parker reminisced in 1956 . . .": Ibid.

21: "And then there's the doctor's house . . .": Dorothy Parker, "Sentiment," *Complete Stories* (New York: Penguin Books, 2005), p. 195.

21: "When Dorothy Rothschild was still . . .": Marion Meade, *Dorothy Parker: What Fresh Hell Is This?* (New York: Villard, 1988), p. 8.

23: "She was crazy . . .": Wyatt Cooper, "Whatever You Think Dorothy Parker Was Like, She Wasn't," *Esquire*, July 1968, p. 57.

24: "If you see any pictures . . .": Dorothy Rothschild, letter to Henry Rothschild, June 1906, collection of Joan Grossman, Nancy Arcaro, Susan Cotton.

25 "Martin Rothschild . . .": Encyclopedia Titanica, http://www.encyclopedia-titanica.org/titanic-victim/martin-rothschild.html

p. 26 "The Majestic was known as 'the Jewish place'...": Michael V. Susi, *The Upper West Side: Postcard History Series* (Chicago: Arcadia, 2009), p. 32.

26: "What is really the keynote . . .": Parker, "An Apartment House Anthology," *Complete Stories*, p. 387.

27: "I am having a lot of fun . . .": Dorothy Rothschild, letter to Henry Rothschild, 1905.

29: "I often wonder why on earth . . .": Stuart Y. Silverstein, ed., *Not Much Fun: The Lost Poems of Dorothy Parker* (New York: Scribner, 1996), p. 94.

31: "The acceptance of the poem . . .": Meade, *What Fresh Hell Is This?* p. 32.

32: "Among her captions were . . .": John Keats, *You Might As Well Live: The Life and Times of Dorothy Parker* (New York: Simon & Schuster, 1970), p. 32.

Chapter 3

36: "You have companionships no . . .": Dorothy Parker, "The Lovely Leave," *Complete Stories* (New York: Penguin Books, 2005), p. 275.

39: "This, no song of an ingénue . . .": Dorothy Parker, *Complete Poems* (New York: Penguin Books, 1999), p. 63.

42: "The term 'the Algonquin Round Table' . . .": Author's interview with Stuart Y. Silverstein.

48: "Plain water in mine . . .": Parker, "Dialogue at Three in the Morning," *Complete Stories*, p. 47.

48: "I lived in a state . . .": Parker, "Soldiers of the Republic," *Complete Stories*, p. 252.

49: "Headquarters was . . .": Parker, "Song of the Shirt, 1941," *Complete Stories*, p. 263.

50: "It is also where . . .": Marion Meade, *Bobbed Hair and Bathtub Gin: Writers Running Wild in the Twenties* (New York: Nan A. Talese/Doubleday, 2004), p. 3.

55: "Lilacs blossom just as sweet . . .": Parker, *Complete Poems*, p. 5.

57: "The roots of Jack and Charlie's . . .": Marilyn Kaytor, *"21": The Life and Times of New York's Favorite Club* (New York: Viking Adult, 1975), p. 13.

58: "With few exceptions the women . . .": Gordon Kahn and Al Hirschfeld, *The Speakeasies of 1932* (New York: Applause Theatre & Cinema Books, 2004.

62: "What are you going to have? . . .": Parker, *Complete Stories*, p. 92.

64: "No more my little song comes back . . .": Parker, *Complete Poems*, p. 6.

67: "Dorothy very ill . . .": Helen Droste, telegram to Seward Collins, March 25, 1927, Seward Collins Papers. Yale Collection of American Literature, Beinecke Rare Book and Manuscript Library.

67: "Seems heart has sprung leak . . .": Dorothy Parker, telegram to Seward Collins, March 30, 1927, ibid.

67: "This is my favorite hospital . . .": Dorothy Parker, letter to Seward Collins, May 5, 1927, ibid.

Chapter 4

Note: All theater reviews in Chapter 4 appear in *The Portable Dorothy Parker* (New York: Penguin Books, 1976), pp. 415-450.

79: "Often in the local press . . .": Stuart Y. Silverstein, ed., *Not Much Fun: The Lost Poems of Dorothy Parker* (New York: Scribner, 1996), p. 113.

81: "Still we're groggy . . .": Silverstein, *The Lost Poems of Dorothy Parker*, p. 115.

83: "I had only one lyric . . .": "Dorothy Parker," in *Writers at Work: The Paris Review Interviews*, ed. Malcolm Cowley (New York: Viking Press, 1957, 1958), p. 76.

Chapter 5

91: "A good many people . . .": Federal Bureau of Investigation, *Report on Dorothy Rothschild Parker*, file 100-56075. Available online at http://foia.fbi.gov/foiaindex/parker_dorothy.htm.

91: "thought we were fools": Marion Meade, *Dorothy Parker: What Fresh Hell Is This?* (New York: Villard, 1988), p. 184.

92: "I was in a brownstone . . .": Randall Calhoun, *Dorothy Parker: A Bio-Bibliography* (Westport, CT: Greenwood Press, 1993), p. 20.

92: "this lotus-laden shore. . . ": Dorothy Parker, "The Passionate Screen Writer to His Love," as cited in Meade, *What Fresh Hell Is This?* p. 277.

95: "People who haven't talked to each other . . .": Robert E. Drennan, *The Algonquin Wits* (Secaucus, NJ: Citadel Press, 1968), p. 116.

95: "In February 1934 . . .": "'Guests' Aiding Strike Beaten at the Waldorf," *New York Times*, February 7, 1934, p. 1.

99: "It was dark outside . . .": Dorothy Parker, *Complete Stories* (New York: Penguin Books, 2005), p. 252.

104: "As the government . . .": Meade, *What Fresh Hell Is This?* pp. 344-45.

104: "to cover a nasty infected eye . . .": "Overflow Rally Spurs Nelson Fight," *Daily Worker*, July 28, 1952.

104: "It's a short step . . .": "A Chat with the Reader," *Daily Worker*, December 27, 1953.

107: "My job was . . .": "Dottie Parker Didn't Ask Where $$ Went," *New York News*, February 26, 1955.

106: "There are things . . .": Dorothy Parker, "The Siege of Madrid," *The Portable Dorothy Parker* (New York: Penguin Books, 1973), p. 589.

Chapter 6

109: "she discovered Alan's body . . .": Marion Meade, *Dorothy Parker: What Fresh Hell Is This?* (New York: Villard, 1988), p. 392.

113: "A housekeeper . . .": Ibid., p. 410.

113: "were not only highly characteristic . . .": Alden Whitman, "Dorothy Parker, 73, Literary Wit, Dies," *New York Times*, June 8, 1967, p. 1.

114: "After Parker's body . . .": Meade, *What Fresh Hell Is This?* p. 412.

117: "In an interview, she said . . .": Author's interview with Marion Meade.

For Further Reading

Polly Adler, *A House Is Not a Home* (New York: Rinehart, 1953).

Sally Ashley, *FPA: The Life and Times of Franklin Pierce Adams* (New York: Beaufort Books, 1986).

Nathaniel Benchley, *Robert Benchley: A Biography* (New York: McGraw-Hill, 1955).

Nat Benchley and Kevin C. Fitzpatrick, *The Lost Algonquin Round Table* (New York: Donald Books, 2009).

Louis Botto, *At This Theatre: 100 Years of Broadway Shows, Stories and Stars* (New York: Applause Theatre & Cinema Books, 2002).

Edwin G. Burrows and Mike Wallace, *Gotham: A History of New York City to 1898* (New York: Oxford University Press, 1999).

Randall Calhoun, *Dorothy Parker: A Bio-Bibliography* (Westport, CT: Greenwood Press, 1993).

Frank Case, *Tales of a Wayward Inn* (New York: Frederick A. Stokes Company, 1938).

Marc Connelly, *Voices Offstage* (New York: Holt, Rinehart and Winston, 1968).

Andrew Dolkart, *Guide to New York City Landmarks* (New York: New York Landmarks Preservation Commission, 2008).

Robert E. Drennan, *The Algonquin Wits* (Secaucus, NJ: Citadel Press, 1968, 1985).

Edward Robb Ellis, *The Epic of New York City* (New York: Marboro, 1966).

Leslie Frewin, *The Late Mrs. Dorothy Parker* (New York: Macmillan, 1987).

James R. Gaines, *Wit's End: Days and Nights of the Algonquin Round Table* (New York: Harcourt, 1977).

Brian Gallagher, *Anything Goes: The Jazz Age Adventures of Neysa McMein and Her Extravagant Circle of Friends* (New York: Random House, 1987).

Jane Grant, *Ross, The New Yorker and Me* (New York: Reynal, 1968).

Margaret Case Harriman, *The Vicious Circle* (New York: Rinehart, 1951).

Sharon Tyler Herbst and Ron Herbst, *The Ultimate A–Z Bar Guide* (New York: Broadway Books, 1998).

Gordon Kahn and Al Hirschfeld, *The Speakeasies of 1932* (New York: Applause Theatre & Cinema Books, 2004).

Beatrice Kaufman and Joseph Hennessey, eds., *The Letters of Alexander Woollcott* (New York: Viking Press, 1944).

Marilyn Kaytor, *"21": The Life and Times of New York's Favorite Club* (New York: Viking Adult, 1975).

John Keats, *You Might As Well Live: The Life and Times of Dorothy Parker* (New York: Simon & Schuster, 1970).

Dale Kramer, *Heywood Broun* (New York: Current Books, 1949).

Marion Meade, *Bobbed Hair and Bathtub Gin: Writers Running Wild in the Twenties* (New York: Nan A. Talese, 2004).

Marion Meade, *Dorothy Parker: What Fresh Hell Is This?* (New York: Villard, 1988).

New Jersey Writers Project, *Entertaining a Nation: The Career of Long Branch* (Long Branch, NJ: Works Projects Administration, 1939).

Dorothy Parker, *Complete Poems* (New York: Penguin Classics, 2010).

Dorothy Parker, *Complete Stories* (New York: Penguin Books, 2005).

Dorothy Parker, *The Portable Dorothy Parker* (New York: Penguin Books, 1944, 1973, 2006).

Robert Miles Parker, *The Upper West Side* (New York: Harry N. Abrams, 1988).

Stuart Y. Silverstein, ed., *Not Much Fun: The Lost Poems of Dorothy Parker* (New York: Scribner, 2009).

Howard Teichman, *George S. Kaufman* (New York: Atheneum, 1972).

James Thurber, *Men, Women, and Dogs* (New York: Harcourt, Brace and Co., 1943).

James Thurber, *The Years with Ross* (New York: Little, Brown, 1959).

James Trager, *The New York Chronology* (New York: HarperCollins, 2003).

E. B. White, *Here Is New York* (New York: Harper & Brothers, 1949; Little Bookroom, 1999).

Edmund Wilson, *The Twenties* (New York: Farrar, Straus and Giroux, 1975).

Peggy Wood, *How Young You Look* (New York: Farrar & Rinehart, 1941).

Ben Yagoda, *About Town: The New Yorker and the World It Made* (New York: Scribner, 2000).

Notable Internet Destinations

- Algonquin Hotel: algonquinhotel.com
- Algonquin Round Table: algonquinroundtable.org
- Natalie Ascencios: ascencios.com
- Cinema Treasures: cinematreasures.org
- City Review: thecityreview.com
- Dorothy Parker Society: dorothyparker.com
- Encyclopedia of Musical Theatre, TV and Film: musicals101.com
- Internet Broadway Database: ibdb.com
- Internet Movie Database: imdb.com
- New-York Historical Society: nyhistory.org
- New York Public Library: nypl.org
- Roaring Forties Press: roaringfortiespress.com
- Robert Benchley Society: robertbenchley.org
- Wit's End, clubwitsend.com

Index

Photography and Illustration Credits

Estate of Franklin P. Adams, courtesy of Tony Adams: pages 46, 57.

Rahne Alexander (rahne.com): page 4.

Natalie Ascencios (ascencios.com): Cover ©2005 Natalie Ascencios, all rights reserved.

Associated Press/Wide World Photos: pages 5 (bottom), 30, 37 (left), 71, 90, 91, 93, 95 (left), 115, 116.

Brown Brothers: pages 25, 32 (left), 37 (right), 50 (right), 53 (top two), 56, 66 (right), 83 (left).

Ellis Butler: page 20.

Clay Enos (clayenos.com): page 146.

Joan Grossman, Susan Cotton, and Nancy Arcaro: page 24 (right).

Paul Katcher (paulkatcher.com): pages 87 (right), 88 (bottom).

Long Branch Historical Association: page 17 (top).

The image on pages 34–35 is copyright MG-AH Operating Inc. Painted by Natalie Ascencios. Photo courtesy of the Algonquin Hotel. At the time of publication, this painting may be viewed in the Algonquin Hotel in Manhattan.

Chris Morgan: page 123 (right).

Mike Owen (livetography.smugmug.com): page 29.

Photofest: pages 2, 10, 16, 18, 19, 22, 52, 53 (bottom), 61 (left), 65 (right), 72, 73, 79 (right), 81 (right), 87 (left), 94 (left), 97 (left), 109, 110, 112 (top right), 124 (right), 126.

Roy Schatt Photo Archive, used courtesy of Elaine Schatt: pages 14, 108.

Don Spiro (donspiro.com): pages 117, 118, 127.

U.S. Department of Justice: pages 96, 102.

U.S. Library of Congress, pages 6 (Prints & Photographs Division, George Grantham Bain Collection [LC-DIG-ggbain-13361]); 7 (Prints & Photographs Division, George Grantham Bain Collection [LC-DIG-ppmsca-06591]); 24 (Prints & Photographs Division, George Grantham Bain Collection [LC-DIG-ggbain-09670]), 26 (LC-USZ62-101589), 43 (Prints & Photographs Division, Carl Van Vechten Collection [LC-USZ62-121914]), 44 (Prints & Photographs Division, Detroit Publishing Co. Collection, [LC-D4-18531]), 50 (left) (Prints & Photographs Division, Detroit Publishing Company Collection [LC-D4-36351]), 54 (Prints & Photographs Division, Detroit Publishing Company Collection [LC-D4-18310]), 68 (left) (Prints & Photographs Division, NYWT&S Collection, [LC-USZ62-124310]), 75 (top left) (George Grantham Bain Collection [LC-DIG-ggbain-35786]), 75 (bottom left) (George Grantham Bain Collection [LC-DIG-ggbain-33081]), 78 (George Grantham Bain Collection [LC-DIG-ggbain-32767]), 79 (left) (Prints & Photographs Division, Detroit Publishing Company Collection [LC-D4-18607]), 80 (left) (George Grantham Bain Collection [LC-DIG-ggbain-35786]), 82 (HABS NY,31-NEYO,104-1), 84 (top) (Prints & Photographs Division, Carl Van Vechten Collection [LC-USZ62-42539]), 88 (right) (LC-USZ62-136509), 89 (LC-DIG-npcc-26935), 106 (LC-USZ62-94413).

All other images are in the author's collection or in the public domain. The author wishes to thank all the photographers and photo researchers who contributed to the success of his book.

Acknowledgments

I wish to acknowledge that this book would not be possible without Susie Rachel Baker, who introduced me to Dorothy Parker; Marion Meade; Roaring Forties Press publishers Deirdre Greene and Nigel Quinney, who put their full trust in me and believed that a website could be the inspiration for a book; Todd Felton, my editor, who made the smooth editorial transition from Transcendentalism to alcoholism; Jeff Urbancic and Karen Weldon, who did such a beautiful job laying out the pages; my supportive parents, Donald and Valerie Fitzpatrick; and Natalie Ascencios; Lawrence Carrel; Carol Butler of Brown Brothers; CBC St. Louis; James X. Dowd; Les Dunseith; Clay Enos; the Long Branch Historical Association; Kate Lynch and bway.net; Ronald Mandelbaum at Photofest; Anthony Melchiorri and the staff of the Algonquin Hotel; Robert Mielke; Paul J. Mineo; Northeast Missouri State University; Kevin O'Sullivan and the Associated Press; Mike Owen; Photofest; Darcie Hind Posz; Elaine Schatt; Stuart Y. Silverstein; David Trumbull and the Robert Benchley Society; Beth Woolley; lice de Almeida, Gary Budge; Paul Katcher; Don Spiro; Wit's End; Flute; Chris Morgan; the Shelter Island Public Library; and my wife, Christina Hensler Fitzpatrick, who didn't know there was another woman in my life when she married me.

About the Author

Kevin C. Fitzpatrick is an independent historian who started the Dorothy Parker Society in 1998. He is a graduate of Northeast Missouri State University and proudly served in the U.S. Marine Corps. After his hitch he entered journalism, working in newspapers, magazines, advertising agencies, and television in Manhattan. Kevin is a licensed New York City sightseeing guide who provides walking tours of city landmarks, cemeteries, and unusual locations. He is a frequent guest speaker at libraries, salons, and private clubs all over New York. In addition to writing *A Journey into Dorothy Parker's New York*, Kevin is coeditor of *The Lost Algonquin Round Table* (Donald Books, 2009). In his spare time he enjoys exploring his family genealogy, collecting comic books, and dedicating bronze plaques to dead people. Kevin and his family split their time between the Upper West Side and Shelter Island.

About the ArtPlace Series

This book is part of the ArtPlace series published by Roaring Forties Press. Each book in the series explores how a renowned artist and a world-famous city or area helped to define and inspire each other. ArtPlace volumes are intended to stimulate both eye and mind, offering a rich mix of art and photography, history and biography, ideas and information. Although the books can be used by tourists to navigate and illuminate their way through cityscapes and landscapes, the volumes can also be read by armchair travelers in search of an engrossing and revealing story.

Other titles include *A Journey into Steinbeck's California, A Journey into the Transcendentalists' New England, A Journey into Matisse's South of France, A Journey into Ireland's Literary Revival, A Journey into Flaubert's Normandy,* and *A Journey into Michelangelo's Rome.*

Visit Roaring Forties Press's website, www.roaringfortiespress.com, for details of these and other titles, as well as to learn about upcoming author tours, readings, media appearances, and all kinds of special events and offers.

A Journey into Dorothy Parker's New York

This book is set in Goudy and Futura; the display type is Futura Condensed. The cover and the interior were designed by Jeff Urbancic, who also made up the pages. Todd Felton served as developmental editor. Sherri Schultz and Michael Carr copyedited the text, which was proofread by Karen Stough and indexed by Sonsie Conroy. Deirdre Greene was the book's editor.